Living Seminole

By Edna Siniff

Water color art and sketches
By Nancy Larkin

ElderBerry Publishing
CMP Publishing Group, LLC

Living Seminole may be ordered directly from your local bookstore.
Edna Siniff
email: ednasiniff@me.com

ElderBerry Publishing
A Division of CMP Publishing Group, LLC
27657 Highway 97
Okanogan, WA 98840

ISBN13: 978-1-937162-12-2

Library of Congress Control Number: 2016931127

Dedication

To my daughters and grand children.

To all the Seminole descendants of those who survived and thrived.

Know that even a child can make a difference.

A Special Thank You

To Nancy Larkin, my high school classmate and close friend who opened her home to me and helped me locate persons who had knowledge from the era I was researching. She also used her talent to create the cover art and sketches for the interior.

To her sister Sharon: who earned a huge thank you for driving me to Big Cypress and contacting Patsy West on my behalf. She also provided other contacts that were extremely helpful.

To Joseph Pillsbury who stepped in at the end to touch up art in preparation for printing and creating chickens for the cover.

To Patsy West for opening her files and archives which provided hard to find documents. And also her supportive conversations. I appreciate her taking time to fact check this manuscript.

To Mary Beth Rosebrough, Research Coordinator at Ah-Tah-Thi-Ki Museum, for her support and for answering my many questions. She also worked to identify individuals in the photos donated to the museum.

I would be remiss if I did not mention author, Milton Meltzer, who wrote "Hunted Like a Wolf." This was the first book I found that documented Josie Billie's story. Meltzer was able to do research in the National Archives, reading documents that I had not been able to access on my travels to Washington, D.C.

To my elementary teacher, Mrs. Hunt/Gilruth, who believed me and called her retired teacher friends, urging them to fight for the Seminole chilcren. She was my hero the day she announced, "Your friends will go to public school." Then continued calling her friends for updates.

Finally to Susie Billie who graciously shared her home with me and allowed me to learn from her the fundamentals so necessary for her existence.

To Josie Billie who challenged me to remember his story and his people with the instruction to return his story, when they were ready to receive it. This book is my commitment to my promise to him.

This "is the way I remember
you...those piercing dark
eyes and broad smile."
Nancy Larkin

Introduction

As an elementary aged child I, with my family, frequently visited the
Dania Seminole Reservation. The City of Dania, Florida, for which
it was named, was nestled between Hollywood and Fort Lauderdale.
While having a busy city center and a large tomato growing
agricultural community it was also the site of Dania Elementary
School. This school played an important role at the beginning of the
Seminole Indian public education process. The tomato fields also
provided employment for many Seminole families.

Dania was home to the Tomato Festival, an event we all looked
forward to each year. A highlight of this event was the annual tomato
fight. Junior and Senior girls and boys lined up behind boxes of
tomatoes well past their prime. Girls against girls and boys against
boys, in turn, drew a raucous crowd. Bleachers on either side of the
arena were filled with shouting spectators. The teams hurled the
squishy fruit at one another until the boxes were empty. All the well-
coated competitors climbed into a large dump truck. The smelly,
jovial bunch were driven to Dania Beach where the truck backed into
the surf and dumped its load. I can cheerfully say that I was one of
the girls sliding into the surf.

This event continued until the Corp of Engineers installed floodgates
on the canals carrying fresh water from the Everglades. These gates,

remained closed most of the time and blocked the manatee from entering the network of canals that supplied their winter food. The gates were closed when the rains produced high water levels, holding the water on the farmland so the cities would not be flooded. This control of fresh water had an adverse affect on the tomato fields. Gradually the seawater infiltrated the porous coral rock foundation under the agricultural lands. The tomato growers had to leave the area to stay in business. Eventually the City of Hollywood expanded to include the area once known as Dania. During this transition Dania Reservation's name was changed to the Hollywood Reservation.

In this book all references to Dania Reservation are understood to be Hollywood Reservation. In reality the change of the reservation's name coincides with the changes that were taking place in the tribal government and the security of its members.

This reservation is contained within 497 acres in Broward County, Florida. The cities of Hollywood and Davie border these acres today. By contrast, Big Cypress covers 81.972 square miles. Brighton Reservation, in central Florida, is 57,090 square miles.

I did not journal as did most of my friends. I kept notes. When an experience held my attention I wrote the facts on notepaper. After the computer became part of my life I began entering my notes into electronic files. These notes provided the nucleus for the story contained in the following pages. The notes could not stand-alone because many of the events were seen from a child's perspective. I could not write about my experiences without documenting them through other sources. The bibliography records the sources that support the stories told me and the experiences that played an important role in developing the person I grew to be.

Table of Contents

Dania Reservation circa 1945

Davie

Dania Seminole Reservation   circa 1945

Future Florida Turnpike

Meeting Chickee

farm house

Infirmary

house

Church

Southern Baptist Mission

Agency

Stirling Road

Chickee

Chickee

Chickee

Chickee

Chickee

Chickee

Chickee

Cemetary

Cemetary

softball field

Cemetary

one room cabins

little selling chickees

State Road No. 7

441

Trading Post and Alligator Pit

to Dania

Giggles and Laughter

Giggles and laughter filled the air as a small group of youngsters cooled under the majestic Oak standing at the edge of a large sandy field. They had been playing a fast moving game of softball.

I was among the Seminole youth gathered in the shade.

Hanging out with the Seminole kids filled my summers and weekends during my elementary school years.

How we found our way to South Florida

Our family moved to Jacksonville, Florida during World War II. Dad was stationed at the naval air base there. At war's end he accepted a job at Hector Supply Company in Miami.

Soon after my family settled into our rental house in Pinewood Park, a suburb of Miami, my mother began driving us to the Dania Reservation (Now Hollywood Reservation.) We spent most of each summer there, free to run and play.

Interaction with children and their parents or guardians was a regular occurrence. We kids functioned like a pack. Our ages ranged from about 7 to about 12. The older ones were always aware of the younger ones and made sure everyone stayed together.

Sometimes we had to go all the way to the edges of the reservation. Each child was given something to carry. We accepted this responsibility with care and with respect for the items we were to deliver. Since we had equal responsibility we each made sure our item arrived safely. Once our packages were delivered chaos broke out. Some kids ran fast to get ahead of the pack. They would hide in or behind a tree ready to jump out to startle the unsuspecting person on the path.

When a heavy vine hung from a tree we would all take turns being jungle kid. We generally ended up running as fast as we could, to report back to the adult who sent us on the errand.

A regular responsibility was raking around the home site. This was done daily. When we weren't helping adults we played games. I ran and played with the kids until I was totally exhausted. They taught me their games, I taught them mine. Often a game was played in the sand with rocks or pieces of wood. A diagram would be drawn for the game. Sometimes it was a version of Hop Scotch other times it would be sets of circles with the objective to throw a stick or stone into a small inner circle. Most of these games were made up on the spot. If they were successful they became part of our game portfolio. When the kids learned a new game, like Rover, Rover, Come Over or Simon Says, the words were very quickly translated into Miccosukee.

Pinecones were often used in throwing and kicking games. And sometimes they were hit with the softball bat or a stick. It was difficult to kick a pinecone if you weren't wearing shoes. I was impressed with the kids who kicked a pinecone barefoot.

The trees were our jungle gym. Most of the kids could swing from branch to branch. The lower branches were used for this game. The branches had to be low enough to jump up and grip and high enough to keep our feet from touching the ground. They also had to be strong enough to hold our weight. Not many trees qualified. Our hands grew strong and tolerant of the rough bark. The kids I ran and played with became my best friends. Before my first summer on the reservation was over we used words from both English and Miccosukee to communicate.

My friend's language was difficult for me to learn because, no matter how hard I tried, I couldn't make some of the sounds. In spite of our differences, we could understand each other perfectly.

Sometimes I could convince the kids to let me read to them. I soon discovered they had no understanding of the activities of "white kids" in the stories. This created lively discussions or arguments. I realized we needed books about and for them. I actually transcribed the story of the first armadillo, given to me by Josie Billie, and illustrated it hoping to make it the beginning of a collection of "Indian" storybooks.

Children who were part of our kid pack.
Edna Siniff (DeHass) photo 1946

Softball

The big game was Softball. Every age was involved at one time or another. We had a girl's and boy's team. Occasionally we mixed them up. Visiting churches supplied the competition. They were raucous, fast moving and fun filled innings. The Seminole kids usually won. When a game was announced spectators drove to the field and piled on the cars, using them for bleachers.

The games were held in the sand lot by the big Oak tree, now the Constitution Tree, near the location of the Hard Rock Hotel and Casino.
Edna, Mr. W.D.DeHass photo Circa 1946

Spectators. Laura Mae on right and Butch on bumper.

Our girls softball team. I loved playing the out field.
Edna, Mrs. W.D.DeHass photos, circa 1946

Another view of members of our team.
Edna, Mrs. W.D.DeHass photo. circa 1946

I don't know how it was possible to catch fly balls with that strange glove, but I did. We were an awesome team. We had little equipment and no uniforms. We wore long pants when we had them. We always played in our street clothes. Who says girls can't play in skirts?

More spectators. It really was the game of choice.
Everyone loved playing and cheering.

Edna, Mrs. W.D.DeHass photos, circa 1946

Swimming

Swimming in the gravel pit was a great, hot afternoon activity.

An old dump truck served as our bus. Everyone, who was able, climbed into the truck's bed for the drive to the clear, clean water that was free from snakes and gators. Most of the participants swam in their clothes because they didn't have swimming suits. Swimming was especially fun when it followed a hot, sweaty softball game.

Some kids even brought soap to wash their bodies and clothes.

Bars of Ivory were preferred because that brand floats. The pit was very deep. No one wanted to dive to the bottom to retrieve a bar of soap.

The washing took place on the side of the pit. The kids would take the soap bar and rub all over their clothes, while wearing them. The more bubbles the better. Every part of their body's would be covered with foam. A friend willingly rubbed the soap over the back of the person next to them. Sometimes two or three kids would be lined up to get soap on their back at the same time.

A good rub created a lot of bubbles. When the kids were sufficiently soapy all would dive in and swim until their clothes and their hair were clear of soap.

Edna Siniff (DeHass) photos circa 1946

Most people I knew thought the tribal members were stoic and had no fun. My friends' public face did not allow their feelings to show. You could say they could put on a "good poker" face. Get them away from the public eye and a whole different persona appears.

Memories of the time we shared on the reservation are the happiest of my childhood.

Visits to the REZ

My parents felt compelled to assist the Seminole Indians of Florida. (1945) The first time we visited the reservation mother became aware of the grave deprivation these tribal members were experiencing. According to the census, at that time, the Florida Seminoles numbered less than 800. These people were hungry and sick. They and their babies were suffering from malnutrition.

Mother began her efforts by coercing the Pinewood Park Baptist Church congregation to collect food and clothing, which my parents transported to the reservation. By summer we were making regular trips with bundles and boxes inside and on top of the old 1936 Ford sedan. Sometimes dad pulled our slat sided trailer filled with "mission boxes." The trips to visit the reservation were always an adventure for my brother and me.

Elementary School

My 4th, 5th and 6th grade school years were at Pinewood Park Elementary School. The small buildings that held individual classrooms and the cafeteria of this school were a collection of individual portable classrooms. The school was created to accommodate the influx of World War II veteran's families with elementary age students.

My first memories of trips to the reservation coincide with my memories of this school. I had the same teacher (Mrs. Hunt/Gilruth) all three years. The first year she had a split class of 3rd and 4th grade. The next year her classroom was 4th and 5th grade. The following year she was my 6th grade teacher. The first year at Pinewood Park Elementary School my teacher's name was Mrs. Gilruth. She remarried during the summer. When we arrived in the fall she wrote Mrs. Hunt on the chalkboard. I preferred saying Mrs. Gilruth. I loved getting that sideways look from her when I "accidentally" reverted to her previous name.

Big Cypress

During my second school year at Pinewood Park Elementary my parents made plans to go to Big Cypress Reservation at the beginning of summer vacation. Anticipation for this trip was more exciting than waiting for Christmas. Mother liked to tell Bible stories, but at this time she was more interested in the needs of the people living in the glades.

Non-Indians rarely faced the complicated task of driving to this remote reservation. There were no roads once you left the two lane paved road.

Dad planned our departure for Big Cypress to coincide with the end of the school year. He had most of the provisions packed and waiting when my brother, Butch, and I walked in the door on our last school day.

The trunk of the car was filled with personal clothing, camping gear and food. Extra gas cans, resting on the back bumper, were tied securely to the trunk hinges.

We left early in the morning. Our car carried our family of four until we reached the Dania Reservation where two women squeezed into our back seat for the ride to Big Cypress. Now we were six. Four adults and two kids compressed in a space designed for four.

We arrived at our rendezvous place around noon. Dad called it the "Jumping Off" spot. As soon as the wheels stopped rolling all four doors swung open and bodies burst out of the cramped space.

Dad had been given a description of the roadside location where the vehicle from the rez would meet us. A huge bank was to our east. It was the dike built on the west side of Lake Okeechobee. The road looked the same as far as the eye could see. Swamp grass to our left and a huge grass covered bank to our right.

"Del, are you sure this is the spot?" queried mother.

"Looks like it. There's the little tree we were told to watch for." The tree he pointed to was a small red cedar type tree, about four feet high. It was the only growth on the bank, other than grass.

Dad looked toward the west and told us to watch the high grass on the horizon.

"You'll see the grass moving when our guide is approaching," he explained.

I sat on the car roof and peered across the high swamp grass for a while then left that perch to climb the high bank, hoping to see the lake. I was partway up the bank when my eye caught something moving off in the distance. It looked like the grass was waving in the wind, but there was no wind. It was our guide. As his pickup truck came closer we could see the grass flattened behind him. This is the trail we would follow to Big Cypress Reservation.

We had to travel during the dry season. We drove through deep sand or mud, around palmetto and tree covered hummocks (islands during the wet season) and small lakes or ponds. It was like driving through new snow. If the vehicle slowed too much the sand or mud sucked the tires in. Getting unstuck required a four-wheel drive tow or a winch with a long cable. Dad always drove on these treks. Mother was co-pilot. She kept track of our progress on hand drawn maps. Our family's only vehicle was a1936 Ford sedan.

Dad often stretched a canvass out from the car to give us shelter from the sun.
Edna Siniff (DeHass) circa 1945

When the guide arrived my brother and I climbed down the short, steep bank to his pick up truck. Mother and the women made their way down the bank also. No one wanted to ride down the steep bank with dad. Our guide watched as he carefully eased the old Ford down the steep slope to the flat land behind his truck. Butch and I rode with the guide, leaving more room for the women in the back seat, on the long ride across the Everglades to Big Cypress.

The trail broken by the pick up, on its way to meet us, opened vistas rarely seen by other than the people who lived in the glades. The swamp grass on either side of us was very high and dry, reaching 12 feet in some places. The grass between the tracks made a musical sound as it rubbed the under side of the truck. We sped along at 15 to 20 miles an hour, slowing only for wildlife that crossed our path. It felt much faster with the tall grass swishing by the sides of the truck. I could see our car in the rear view mirror. Dad stayed close.

Birds of all kinds lifted from the trees on the hummocks we passed. Ibis and eagles were common. Many of the trees were filled with small perching birds. Deer crossing our path moved into the tall grass before we reached them.

Our guide talked to Butch and I all the way to Big Cypress, pointing out things that might interest two kids. Islands in the mass expanse of swamp grass were covered with trees. "We call those hummocks," he explained. Some of those trees were orange trees. Not the cultivated type, but wild oranges that were pithy and dry. "Good food but not much taste," he told us.

"You will like the snails," he said. "They have pretty colored bands. The snails living on the trees in each hummock have their own color pattern." He went on to explain how hunters in the glades knew where they were by the colored bands on the snails. We wanted to stop and look at them. "Not now, maybe another time."

The sun set before we reached our destination. There was no moon. It was very dark after the sun went down. The headlights provided a ribbon of light in front of us. As we rounded a curve in the grass path the headlights shown on a large black cat like creature.

"What's that?" I asked.

"A panther," answered our guide.

The cat's coat glistened in the glow from our headlights. Its muscles rippled under its skin as it moved across the opening ahead of us.

"Beautiful," I sighed.

Just before the panther entered the tall grass he turned his head toward us. His eyes reflected emerald green. I had just witnessed a sighting of one of the last remaining true Florida Black Panthers.

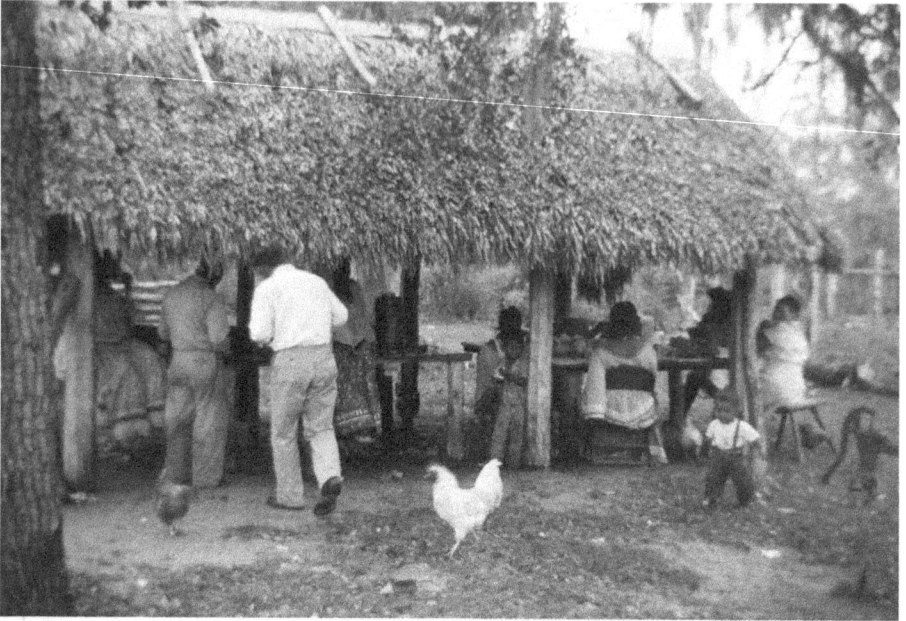

The eating chickee at Big Cypress
W.D.DeHass photo, circa 1946

The people of Big Cypress prepared chicken and kalu, and fry bread ready for us. **Food was cooked over a wood fire.**

W.D. DeHass photo, circa 1946

It had been a long day without eating. My brother and I were famished.

A kettle of sofkee simmered on the fire. Sofkee was a new experience for me. (Corn meal cooked to a smooth drink). Eventually I learned to appreciate and love the nourishing liquid. Kalu prepared in the fry pan on the open fire and the fry bread served with it were delicious.

Kalu was the Seminole word for a small, white, wading bird in the Heron family. The Wood Ibis or sometimes the Cattle Egret were the wild birds of choice for food. It was prepared in the same way as chicken.

Dad packed hammocks as sleeping bunks for Butch and I. He strung them between trees and hung mosquito nets over them. The hammocks were Navy surplus from World War II and the nets were Army camouflage. The combination made a cozy nest for each of us. My parents used an old scout tent and cots.

The next day, Dad and Mom had meetings with the Tribal members. My parents had come to learn their needs. This was a very remote community. After their experiences at Dania they were prepared for the worst. Finding these famlies healthier, with a good food supply, was a great relief to them.

Big Cypress was quite different from Dania. The land on this reservation had good soil where gardens were growing. They raised corn, squash and potatoes. There was an abundance of wildlife. Hogs, cattle and chickens provided food as needed.

Of course, Mother always ended their meetings with a bible study. She told bible stories with a flannel graph. The scenes she painted on large flannel pieces were beautiful. She cut and painted her characters on paper then glued flannel cloth on the back. Her figures were large enough to be seen from the last circle of those, sitting on the ground. After her stories, the women gathered around the easel to touch the fabric. They would take one of the figures off the scene and study it front to back. Mother would turn the figure over in their hands and rub the back, then rub the fabric on the board. "Flannel sticks to flannel." The women played with the figures, moving them from place to place. Giggles erupted as they understood the concept.

Mother and Child in Big Cypress Circa 1946

W.D.DeHass photo

While my parents talked with the adults Butch and I explored with the kids. Big Cypress seemed to be an island of high land in the middle of the everglades. Groups of large trees interspersed with open fields of corn or other gardens gave a patchwork pattern to the landscape. Pitcher pumps were located near some of the camps. A water faucet at the Indian Agency building also provided safe, fresh water. Lots of farm animals shared the land with the people. Hogs and chickens wandered freely. The cattle were in a large herd grazing on the grassland. All the homes were chickees. These homes were scattered over the Big Cypress area. Acres of trees surrounded each family's camp (home site), providing privacy and protection from storms. There were no obvious bathrooms or bathing facilities.

Dirt roads led to each family's camp. We kids ran on the tire paths.

The corn field had been picked when we arrived. The best growing season for this crop was during the winter/spring months. Ears of corn, woven together by leaves of their husks hung in the tops of the cooking chickees.

We ran past tomato plants with ripe fruit and some kind of squash. Some of the growing things were being eaten by the hogs and chickens.

All the adults were gathered near the church. A large outdoor area served as their meeting place. Tall oak type trees provided shelter from the sun. Adults, with their children, sat on the ground to listen and speak. This is also where we sat to eat our meals when it was dry.

The people willingly shared their concerns with Mother. After the meetings, Dad often spent time with the men and their vehicles. Dad was an excellent mechanic. Many times he was able to solve a mechanical problem with them.

As long as they had money to purchase fuel for their vehicles and ammunition for the rifles they could survive very well.

Big Cypress, it seemed, was the supporting food source for the Dania families. The problem they continued to experience was transportation from this location. Big Cypress was only accessible, by autos, during the dry season. Getting their food from this isolated reservation to the hungry families at Dania required money for gas. Money was short for all the tribal members at this time.

Monsoon Rains

Early in the afternoon clouds began to build up. About 2 p.m. an elder came to my father and told him if he needed to get back to Dania, he had better leave right away. "The rains are coming," he explained, "and once they start it may be weeks before we can get you out." We had only been in Big Cypress one day.

The announcement was followed by urgent preparations to leave. The ones who absolutely had to get out rode in the first vehicles of the caravan. Dad and mom were at the front of the line, right behind the lead car. Those vehicles were full when we reached them. Dad told us to get in one of the other vehicles. "We'll find a place for you when we get to the road."

My brother and I walked to each vehicle in the line. Eight in all. Each car or truck was filled to capacity. At the end of the line stood the big Russian Jeep. That is what my brother and I called this giant World War II surplus vehicle. It was empty. We climbed in.

The giant jeep was the support vehicle for any that mired in the muck or stalled along the way. The tires were as tall as my shoulders. My brother pushed me up and I gave him a hand as he clambered over the tires. We settled into the back seat and waited for the driver.

The rains began to fall as the caravan pulled out. Our driver asked if we really wanted to leave Big Cypress. My brother and I looked at each other and smiled. "Are you kidding?" Butch answered. We had just arrived, now we had to leave. We didn't want to go home. Our driver made a valiant effort to get us to the highway, but the rains came fast. This was an open vehicle. The raindrops were huge and stung as they pounded on our skin. It was a monsoon type rain. Water on our path raised quickly. Many of the cars in the caravan were struggling to reach the highway. Some stalled in the deepening water. Traveling together, helping each other, kept everyone safe. Our driver had helped get some of them out of sticky sand. He stayed behind the last vehicle until he saw its taillights moving out of sight. Our vehicle couldn't go as fast as the smaller cars. The dark, water filled clouds blocked out the sun. Darkness closed in rapidly. There was no twilight as the sun set. Suddenly our driver stopped. Our front wheels were on the verge of rolling into a lake. He looked at us and winked. "It looks like you are going to get your wish." He turned the giant four-wheel drive jeep around and headed back to Big Cypress. It took us longer to get back because all the trails were now several feet under water and it was pitch black. The wind-driven rain made it difficult to see anything. Our headlights reflected on the water ahead of us. He drove slowly, feeling his way back to solid ground.

The caravan of vehicles struggled on without us. I can only imagine how Mother and Dad felt when they pulled onto the paved road and discovered Butch and I weren't in any of the vehicles.

We had spent enough time with the Seminole families at Dania that a trust had built between us. Mother and Dad also had a very strong faith in God. I know the people who drove out with my parents reassured them that their children would be well cared for. All the people depended on each other for survival. All shared their resources. Children from Dania families often spent time at Big Cypress. None of us thought the separation would be very long.

Once the giant jeep reached the high ground on the Big Cypress Reservation our driver drove directly to Josie Billie's camp. When we arrived he got out and talked to Josie and Susie Billie quietly. My brother and I strained to hear what they were saying, but their words eluded us. Josie and Susie asked the driver to leave me at this camp. My brother was taken to a family with boys his age. We arrived with only the clothes on our backs. During the time we lived, as guests, in Big Cypress we did not see each other. The families lived too far apart.

I was soaked to the skin and a bit chilled from the pounding rain. Susie took me inside the chickee, rubbed my hair and face with a soft piece of fabric. With her arm around me she lead me to the fire in the cooking chickee. She gave me a cup of sofkee and a piece of fry bread. Susie's gentleness made me feel secure. My clothes dried as I sat by the fire. When it was time to go to bed Susie wrapped a blanket around me and walked me to the platform that would be my sleeping space.

I knew I was an unexpected guest and no one knew how long I would be with them. From the first moment in the Billie camp I knew I was in a very special place. I respected and admired them and realized I would live here until the water receded and the trail to the road dried

Using the pestle and mortar in Susie Billie's camp.

Edna Siniff (DeHass) photo Circa 1946

out enough to support a vehicle.

Josie Billie was an Elder and a healing person. Susie was also a healer. This was the beginning of a long and special friendship. Learning how to live in a Seminole camp in the everglades impacted my life and my future.

The Billie's lived in a chickee, as did most of the Seminoles at that time. This chickee had ten poles holding up the roof—four on each sides and one on each end to hold the edges away from the living area. Even I had to duck my head as I entered the chickee. This design prevented blowing rain from reaching the living space on the platforms. The roof was covered with palmetto thatch. There were two platforms about four feet off the ground. One was used for sleeping and the other was a work area where Susie Billie did her sewing and made baskets. At night I slept among her sewing things on the second platform. There was a space about three or four feet wide between the two platform areas. Large pieces of cloth were dropped down at night making two large private rooms. The heavy rains made everything feel damp but when the cloth dropped each night the sleeping area felt quite cozy.

The damp air was filled with the natural fragrances of the different species of trees and shrubs mixed with the aroma of the slowly cooling embers in the fire.

A natural fear of snakes haunted me that first night in the chickee. My imagination ran wild and filled me with apprehension.

Snakes can climb!

They might want to sleep with me!

I lay in my cozy nest shivering from snake fear. Then I realized there was a hog under my platform. She was rubbing her side on the post supporting my resting place. She immediately became my friend. I was happy to feel her beneath my bed.

Hogs, I knew, ate snakes!

I rolled over and fell asleep, knowing my guardian was under me.

The first morning, after waking, Susie took me into the woods nearby and showed me the tree that would mark my bathroom while I lived with her. She gave me a flattened stick that served as my digging tool to prepare a hole to receive my deposits. She also showed me which leaves were safe to use as tissue. I loved camping. Taking care of ones waste was familiar to me. Learning that I would have privacy was important. Each person, explained Susie, has their own tree. She conveyed to me that respect fore each person's private space was very important.

There was no electricity, no refrigeration, no radio and worst of all, no books. The only things I missed were library books. The rising and setting sun determined our working and sleeping times.

Each morning when I awoke, Susie had a fire going for cooking breakfast. The fire pit was protected by a small chickee, open on both ends to allow the smoke to easily escape. There was always a kettle of sofkee on the fire. This was made by boiling hand ground corn meal. Hot water was also boiling for coffee or what I called, swamp tea. The flat bread left from the night before completed our breakfast.

I helped Susie after breakfast. We used a wood mortar made from a large cypress log to grind the dried corn. The top of the log was carved with sloping sides the shape of a bowl. A hole the size of the pestle was at the bottom of the bowl. The corn kernels slid into the hole as the pestle was raised. The pestle was a pole about four feet long and five inches thick. It took about thirty minutes of pounding to grind corn for the day.

The ground corn was put through three different sieves that nested together for storage. The first sieve had the largest holes. The corn left in it usually went back in the mortar or was fed to the chickens and hogs. The remainder in the second sieve was used to make Sofkee. The finer powder from the final sieve was used in the bread Susie baked by the fire. Corn was grown in a field near the home site. It had been harvested and stored before I arrived. Many ears were hanging in the rafters of the cooking chickee.

When chicken was on the menu, the bird had to be caught, slaughtered, plucked, and cleaned before cooking. We planned ahead when Susie wanted chicken. During the day she would point out the bird she wanted. In the evening, when the birds had gone to roost, I would quietly lift the bird from its perch in the tree. A small cage contained the bird over night. She hung the cage on a stub of a branch protruding from on the underside of the roof in the cooking chickee.

Most of the time the meat for the meal was wild. Fish and Kalu were the most commonly served. Kalu was perfectly suited for feeding a family. One bird, one family meal, no waste. This was important because, without refrigeration, any meat left over would spoil before the next meal-time arrived.

The meals were created around the natural things growing in the everglades. A variety of wild orange trees grew near the chickee. This fruit was nourishing even though it had little juice. Guavas were everywhere. This extremely nourishing food tasted better to me when I was hungry. Palmetto heart was quite tasty. I loved it. Some grains new to me were cooked in a broth made from the meat that was cooking. Potatoes growing in the gardens were served often. These were boiled or fried. Susie rarely used canned beans, peas or tomatoes. Canned goods were precious. They were expensive and had to be carried many miles.

Each day we gathered starter wood, chopped it into usable pieces and stacked it close to the fire. We carried clean water from the faucet at the Indian Agency house, fed the hogs and chickens, raked the ground under and around the living area, washed clothes and left the whole area clean and organized.

There was plenty of natural foods for the chickens and hogs. Susie fed them a little cracked corn each day to keep them close to the camp. The hogs rooted around the small plants in the trees. The chickens ate insects and small creatures. This natural food made them taste wonderful when cooked. No seasoning was necessary.

Clothing was washed by pounding with a stick a couple of inches in diameter. I couldn't believe how clean the cloth became with only pounding and dipping the garment in water. If there was a stubborn spot a bar of hard soap was rubbed on it before pounding. The board on which the clothing rested while pounding was about the size of an old fashioned washboard. After rinsing, the pieces were draped over the long grasses to dry.

When all the chores were completed Susie began sewing. Her sewing machine had a crank on the drive wheel. She would sit cross-legged with the machine on the platform in front of her. Susie cranked with the right hand and fed the fabric with her left. She taught me how to tear the long strips, stitch and cut, stitch and cut, etc. to make many different designs. She was a very clever woman. Her choices of colors made striking designs. Today these designs are called patchwork. To Susie and I they were designs.

Josie Billie had many obligations so was gone much of the time. Occasionally he took me along when he was gathering his healing herbs and plants. He showed me how to pick the leaves so that none of the essence was lost. I learned to recognize the leaves for tea, and would gather them on my own, sometimes. Everything Josie looked at or collected was fascinating to me. I asked a lot of questions. He answered them patiently when they warranted an answer.

One day, after breakfast, I visited my tree then went for a walk to see how far the water had risen. About 500 feet from my tree I saw a boy child's shirt lying on the ground. Thinking it was lost I brought it back to the camp. The look on Susie's face told me I had done something very wrong. "I can take it back to the spot. I know exactly where it was," I stammered. Susie explained that this garment was left for the spirit of the small boy who died. I was devastated. She went on to explain my responsibility to that small spirit.

Two Monkeys

Susie spoke Miccosukee. Thanks to my playmates on the Dania Reservation I could speak a few words and could understand a lot of what Susie said.

I loved to sew, but all the sewing I had done previously required the use of a pattern. One day, while working on the platform with Susie, she reached into a bundle and pulled out a pattern.

"Can you show me how to use this?"

"Yes," I answered. I had been using patterns to make doll clothes since I was five years old. I loved sewing pieces of fabric together to create new things.

The pattern in her hand was for a small stuffed monkey. I showed her the information on the back of the envelope. Then pointed to the numbers under the heading: Items Needed. The amount of fabric needed to make one monkey's body was ¼ yard. It also listed how many inches were needed for the face, inside the ears and the palms of the hands and feet.

I flattened the pattern pieces on the wood platform then touched the edge and seam line to show her the seam allowance and where the pattern directed you to sew with the machine. The little arrows on the curve were guides to line up the cut pieces for sewing. The long arrows on each piece showed the straight of fabric directions. I pulled a piece of fabric to demonstrate the straight. Susie understood.

We both began looking through her bundles of cloth and old clothing for a scrap of brown large enough to make two monkeys. At the bottom of one pile of discarded clothing we found an old pinwhale corduroy skirt with pieces large enough to cut bodies, heads, arms, legs and tails for two monkeys.

The pattern for the face was missing. Susie gave me a pencil and a brown paper bag to create the missing pattern pieces. Though it wasn't perfect, we had a pattern to work from.

Pink felt, used as backing for some of Susie's bead work, was cut for the face and palms of hands and feet

We laid the pattern pieces on the corduroy and began cutting. We were like two little schoolgirls giggling and laughing the whole time. After the required work was done each day we worked on our monkeys.

Each section was sewn separately then stuffed. An old car seat discarded in the woods provided high quality stuffing. We had to dig past the torn part to find clean, dry cotton.

As our monkeys took shape our giggles grew louder turning into downright laughter. It is good no one was nearby; we might have had a crowd watching us.

Then, one day all the parts were sewn together and two cute monkeys sat in front of us. Susie took out her bead box. Small black beads were chosen to sew on for eyes. A small strip of red felt became the mouth on each stuffed animal. They were done!

I still have my monkey. Perhaps somewhere on this earth my monkey's brother still exists.

Josie Billie as a Teacher

While living in the glades I missed the stories books provide. When Josie was around I begged him to tell me stories. I could understand him. He spoke English, Miccosukee, Muscogee and Creek. His English was very good.

Because I missed reading so much I asked Josie to tell me stories. He told me many different tales. Some were history and some were examples of their spirituality. Sometimes I had trouble understanding all he said because he would change languages. He spoke to me in English most of the time. If he used Miccosukee I could understand him, but when he spoke Creek or Muscogee the words became a jumble.

Josie told me how his ancestors left the Creek Nation because the land in that part of the country was getting too crowded. He described the large gardens and farms his people inhabited north of Lake Okeechobee after they arrived in the land now called Florida. How their log homes were built near the gardens and how all the people worked on the land and helped plant the seeds and roots and watered the growing things. He talked about the large herds of cattle and other "farm" animals. He described the villages. He told how they were governed by chosen leaders and rules created by his people. He told me about the War years and the Seven Year War and the treachery used against his people to move them from their homeland. Each day I learned more of their history.

One night Josie Billie asked me to sit by the fire after dinner. We were sitting on the logs by the cooking fire when he started to tell me stories. He began with stories for the children—Tales that helped them learn their culture and behaviors.

Josie Billie's Children's Story

"There was a lady fox who was very proud of her coat. She walked with pride through the grasses, around the hummocks and over the trails. One day she went to the lake near her den, took off her beautiful coat, hung it over a branch and entered the water to bathe.

Lady Fox lay back in the water and swirled it with her hands, making her turn slowly. She looked up at the clouds and saw images in them. While studying the clouds she heard a noise. Quickly she put her feet down and looked around.

There on a log lay a large turtle. He had been there all morning. Lady Fox did not see him when she took her beautiful coat off and hung it on the tree. Thinking the big male turtle had been watching her she became furious.

Quickly she crawled out of the water and put on her beautiful coat. Fastened it up tight and ran around the lake to where the turtle was sleeping. Her shouting woke him up. "You can't watch me bathe," she yelled.

Turtle slid into the water and sank to the bottom of the lake. Lady Fox stood on the log and waited for him to come up for air. When his head popped up she grabbed for him. Turtle pulled his head into his shell just as her mouth closed. Turtle swam as fast as he could toward a little piece of land that protruded into the lake. Fox ran around the edge of the water to reach him before he crawled into the low brush under the trees. It was a long way around the lake. Turtle crawled into the bushes and stayed very quiet.

Lady Fox found his trail and sniffed all around. She knew exactly where the turtle crawled. The bushes were so tight she couldn't get through. Turtle saw her and pushed his shell through the low branches looking for a safe place to hide.

Lady Fox jumped up and down trying to find an opening in the bushes. She didn't want to get burs in her beautiful coat or catch it in the branches. Frantically she ran back and forth.

Turtle pushed harder and harder, getting farther and farther from Lady Fox. Lady Fox heard him moving deeper into the hummock. She ran along the low bushes, jumping up to look for Turtle. She jumped and ran until she reached the other side of the hummock.

Turtle was covered with dead grasses and twigs that stuck to his shell as he pushed through the bushes. He was getting very close to the edge of the hummock. Lady Fox heard Turtle and started shouting at him again. "You can't watch me bathe. I will tear you to pieces."

Turtle stopped moving. He was very frightened. He looked for a place to hide. The sun was setting. It would be dark soon. The moon would be very small. Maybe he could find a safe place to hide.

Lady Fox curled up next to the bushes and went to sleep. She dreamed of catching that terrible turtle and tearing him apart.

When the sun came up the next morning Turtle was moving again. He headed in another direction. Lady Fox stirred when she heard the bushes rustling. "I'll catch you," she shouted.

Two more days passed with Turtle crawling under the bushes and Lady Fox jumping and shouting at him.

On the third day the turtle came to a large log with a hole all the way through it. He crawled in as far as he could go. He didn't see that the log was on the edge of the hummock. He crawled so far into it that he was nearly at the other end.

Lady Fox got very quiet. She sniffed and sniffed. He's close, I know he is close, she thought. Then she came to the end of the log where he was hiding. Fast as a rabbit she put her head into the log, grabbed Turtle by his foot and dragged him out. She shook him. She tossed him against the log. Grabbed him over and over until there was nothing but pieces all over the ground.

Lady Fox stood back. She was really tired. She looked at the pieces of Turtle and announced, "That will teach you not to look at a lady while she bathes." She brushed her beautiful coat and proudly walked away.

When Lady Fox was out of sight the Ant People came out from under the leaves and twigs and began gathering Turtle's pieces. All day they worked to put him back together. When the Ant People were finished they stood back to look at their work. Turtle was different.

Turtle wasn't a turtle any more.

He was the First Armadillo.

Josie told me this story many different times. Each time there was a different lesson.

The floodwaters, that separated our vehicle from the others in the caravan the day the clouds burst open and drenched us, were gradually going down. I knew when the trail to the highway was dry enough to support a car that I would be going home. I loved spending my days with Susie. The Billie chickee was a wonderful, secure home for me.

Shortly before it was time for me to leave Josie told me his grandfather's story. When he finished he had me repeat it to him, until I had it correct. After I had all the events in the proper order, he gave me instructions. "You can't change any part of it." Then his head dropped, a tear came to his eye. "My Indians don't want this story. Someday they will and you will give it to them."

"How will I know when it is time to give it back?"

"You will know," he replied.

Writing this book is my effort to keep the promise I made, as a child, to Josie Billie on that August day so long ago.

Josie Billie's Grandfather's Story

There were many tribes living in Florida when the first white man came. We were not called Seminole. Each tribe had its own name. I am from the Creek.

We didn't live in chickees like this. (He waved his arm denoting the chickee we were in.) We lived in wood houses. We lived in villages on good land. We had large gardens where we grew corn, beans and squash. The whole village worked in the gardens. We dried the grains and ground them. We hunted for wild meat.

When the Spanish came they brought live food; Cattle, chickens, sheep and pigs. We gathered the cattle they left behind and began raising them. We had large herds of cattle before the soldiers came. We were a happy people.

When the soldiers came they destroyed our fields. They burned our homes. They stole our cattle. They forced us off our good land. We defended our land. The Seminole wars went on for many years.

We fought the soldiers. In the beginning we didn't have guns like the soldiers. We used bows and arrows and knives. We knew where the soldiers would walk. Our men hid along those trails. Some were high in the trees using birdcalls to tell us where the Soldiers were. We would quietly take the last man in the line. Our strength was greater than his. We would pull him into the palmetto. Before he knew what happened the soldier was dead. We would take everything we could use from him. We did this over and over.

When the soldiers started to attack our families we moved the women and children, and the elders south of where the Tamiami Trail is today. There was a large island in the swamp that was completely surrounded by wet sand that no man or animal could pass over. There was one narrow place that had ground strong enough to support a man. The width of that trail was about two feet. The wet sand came up to our knees when we walked on the trail. We took everything from the villages to this island. We kept our families there for many years. The soldiers never found this place.

The Seven Years War ended when the general promised us we could live

38

on our land in peace. He invited us to Tampa Bay to celebrate the end of the war. He had a big boat. We were told the feast was on the boat. When all of the Indians were on the boat, the soldiers pulled up the anchor and sailed away. We were trapped. Some young men jumped off the boat and began swimming to shore. The soldiers shot them.

The boat stopped when it came to New Orleans. More soldiers came around us. They pushed and shoved us to make us walk. We walked to Oklahoma. Many of my people died on the way. Oklahoma was not a good place for us. Many of my people walked back to Florida. Strong young men and women would follow the trail towards the Gulf [of Mexico]. They walked along the shoreline, in the marshes, until they were home. Many of my people stayed in Oklahoma.

Josie and I had many conversations about his people and the wars. I couldn't wrap my mind around the cruelty. During one of those conversations he told me about the Caluse people.

"One of the tribes living here was the Caluse. (Calusa) The Caluse made large canoes. They were seagoing people. They went to the islands in the Caribbean and around the gulf waters to all the tribes. They traveled up the coast of Florida, as far north as North Carolina. The Caluse traded with other tribes. They brought seeds and things that we could use. They carried information to all the people on their travels. They told us the white man made slaves of the peoples on the islands and that many were killed.

Time to go Home

I was sad when the rains stopped falling. I knew my time in Big Cypress was coming to an end. I did not want to go home. Josie and Susie made me feel special. I was treated with respect and love. I loved and respected them. I knew my parents would not understand any part of my wonderful experience.

The day came for us to leave. My brother and I climbed into the Russian Jeep again and our driver headed out. I waved goodbye to my new family. Tears were in our eyes, but, joy was in my heart because I had two very special friends. They sent me home with a set of sieves woven by Susie and a sofkee spoon carved by Josie.

Living in the Billie Chickee was the beginning of a long and special friendship. Jose and Susie probably didn't know how much they impacted my life, my future, and my love and respect for the Seminole people. The education I received that summer has served me well.

The flood waters caused the tall grasses to fall. New grasses were beginning to grow through their dead and tangled remains. It was easy to see the hummocks and how they spotted the horizon. The Everglades was beginning a new chapter of growth, as was I.

Mother and Dad were happy to have us home, but were not willing to hear our stories. I think, in some ways they were jealous of our experiences.

At home I began looking for documents to support Josie's story. I believed the general population would not accept Josie's oral history without documentation. Using the National Archives and recorded early observations by Hernando de Soto and William Bartram I began to verify Josie's story. Both of these men recorded aspects of the native populations in Florida that matched Josie Billie's descriptions of his people.

Desoto traveled through the southern region of the future United States in the mid 1500s and William Bartram, a trained natural scientist from Philadelphia, in the 1770s.

In 1973, while searching the history section in our local library, I was thrilled to find Milton Meltzer's book "Hunted Like a Wolf, The story of the Seminole War." This well-documented book is filled with confirmations of the story Josie Billie told me so many years earlier. Meltzer included Bertram's descriptions and drawings from his fieldwork in the mid 1770s. He describes the Seminole village in much the same way as Josie. His drawings made me feel like Josie had stood in that village when he was describing it to me.

It thrilled me to read Hernando de Soto's arrival in Tampa Bay in 1539. *With about six hundred soldiers and a few women, his army headed north on mules and horses, driving before them their live food supply—poultry, pigs, sheep and cattle.* There was Josie's live food and the start of the Seminole cattle herds that would be stolen years later. Josie's oral history matched the written history from 1539.

 Toward the end of Meltzer's book a description from the National Archives tells of the invitation to a Feast at the end of the war that lasted seven years. Halleck's band escaped the final intense attack by Field Commander Colonel Worth's troops. Two weeks later Halleck, knowing he could not continue to fight, came in under a flag of truce. He was moved to a new location while a messenger was sent to his band to invite them to a feast at Warm Springs. In the midst of the festivities soldiers encircled them, loaded them on wagons and rushed them to Tampa Bay to board a ship to New Orleans.

We know the documents in the National Archives about the Indian Wars are mostly written by the military. It is safe to assume both endings are correct. The Indians were invited to a feast in peace. While enjoying the celebration they were surrounded by armed military and forced to leave their homeland.

Education

Coming home to my family was bitter-sweet. Mother immediately took the sofkee spoon and sieves from me. Her intention was to keep them safe. Many years later I saw the sofkee spoon in the family bookcase. I never saw the sieves again.

My parents and I never discussed my time in the Everglades nor did we talk about their feelings when they discovered Butch and I didn't make it out during the heavy rains. I know they were worried. I also know their faith in God and their trust in the Seminole people gave them strength. On the few occasions a reminder of our time in Big Cypress surfaced Mother would say, "You were in God's hands. We knew you were safe."

Mother expressed concern when I told her I wanted to tell my school friends about living in the glades. She admonished me and told me to never speak about it with anyone. She explained that many people in our neighborhood would not feel kindly toward me if they knew I had lived with Seminoles.

Why?

Mother explained her reason. "Because we live in a very segregated state. Many people still feel animosity toward the Seminoles." She believed someone would harm me if they knew how much I cared about my Seminole friends.

Nonetheless my parents still felt compelled to assist the Seminole Indians of Florida. Their visit to Big Cypress left them more determined to help the people on the Dania Reservation.

Now that my brother and I were home from Big Cypress we again enjoyed our frequent trips to the Dania Reservation. It was mid-August. I was excited about the pending start of the new school year. My friends on the reservation seemed uneasy. Charlotte Tommie, my best friend, didn't want to talk about school. I didn't understand why she seemed uneasy about going to school. I loved school and wanted them to enjoy it too.

A few days later the ringing of the phone summoned my Mother.

As she placed the phone in its cradle she shouted to me. There was urgency in her voice.

"We have to leave right NOW. The bus has come for the children. If you want to say goodbye we have to go."

"What bus? Who?" I asked as we got in the car.

"Your playmates on the Reservation." Mother was driving much too fast.

"Not Charlotte," I pleaded.

"Yes, she is going too."

When my mother and I arrived at the parking area behind the Agency building, a large school bus was waiting. Parents and younger children were standing close together. All my friends were on the bus. Waving hands stretched out of the windows. I ran to the bus where their outstretched arms were reaching toward me.

"Where are you going?"

"To school in North Carolina. We'll see you next summer if we can come home." Their hands strained to reach mine as I jumped to touch their fingers.

They were going to ride a yellow school bus all the way to the Cherokee Indian School in North Carolina. Now I knew why they had been so uneasy. I found Charlotte's mother.

"Please don't send Charlotte away," I begged. I dropped to my knees and was hugging her legs.

"Please!"

Her mother's gentle hands brushed the hair from my face and rubbed the tears from my eyes.

"Charlotte has to go to North Carolina. It is the only way she can go to school."

"Let her go with me."

Tears were flowing down our faces as we hugged. With her lips near my ear she whispered,

"Seminole children aren't allowed to go to your schools."

I was devastated.

My heart broke as the bus pulled away. The sad faces of the parents and the brave faces of the children sadly looking out the bus windows would be forever etched in my memory.

Josie's story flashed through my mind. My youthful thoughts made a comparison. My friends are being shanghaied, just like their ancestors,

On our way home my mother was very quiet. She had no answers for my questions. As my anger grew I began to shout.

"If Charlotte can't go to school, I won't go."

"That's not an option." My mother was speaking in a calm voice. "The laws that keep Charlotte from going to your school, require you to attend."

"It's not fair," I shouted.

In the silence that followed my last outburst I was trying to think of a way to help Charlotte and the rest of my friends to come home. As an almost eleven-year-old there seemed to be no options open to me or to the kids on that bus. It all seemed hopeless.

Only my sobs broke the silence as we traveled home.

I decided I had to do something. It wasn't fair that my friends had to leave home to go to school. I tried to imagine what it would be like to not have parents or siblings around me.

As I rode in silence I remembered my dad and I sitting on the steps at the Indian Agency. Dad taught me that silent, persistence can create change. I sat with him on the Dania Seminole Indian Agency steps when the Agent refused to talk to him about bathrooms and clean water for the Seminole people on that reservation.

We sat on the steps outside the door for days staring at the many oak trees that protected us from the sun. The ground under those trees was bare. There was no support for grass or small plants in the sandy soil. Dad talked about that ground being perfect for a building with toilets and showers.

Everyone entering the building had to step over us. We stayed calm and quiet. Dad chuckled when he told me, "We'll just be a thorn in their foot." Finally the Agent came out and asked Dad what he had in mind. Dad pulled a paper from his pocket, explaining that the people living on this reservation needed clean water and bathrooms. Dad believed a building with flush toilets, showers and faucets for filling water jugs could be built. I don't know what other influences came to bear on the Indian Agent that caused him to agree to have the building constructed. He promised dad that he would look into the matter. In my child's mind, my dad and I caused the facility to be built even though it would be years before we would see an actual building.

I had seen quiet rebellion cause action so I decided I would quietly fight for my Seminole friends. We were nearly home when I told Mother, "You can make me go to school, but you can't make me learn." I began dreaming of a day when all the Seminole children would attend schools close to their homes.

Overview of American Indian Education

American Indian Education began in earnest when representatives of various religious denominations were sent to the reservations to rid them of their native culture by converting them to Christianity. By the late 1800s Bureau of Indian Affairs officials promoted sending the American Indian children to boarding schools off the reservation. In these schools the young students would be taught English and to renounce their culture as well as teaching them reading, writing and arithmetic. Lt. Richard Henry Pratt in Pennsylvania, established this system when he opened the Carlisle Indian School.

By 1885 The Bureau of Indian Affairs established its Education Division. Now the efforts to educate the younger American Indians in reading, writing, and arithmetic also included agriculture, domestic skills and mechanical training. All of the schools available to Indian students were boarding schools and required the students to leave their families and their culture.

In all, there were around 500 boarding schools. Cherokee Indian School to which many Florida Seminole students were sent was one of the 500. In addition to boarding schools, day schools were established on or near some reservations.

The Indian Reorganization Act of 1934 passed, giving the Tribes greater autonomy. In essence allowing the tribes to determine where their children went to school and what they were taught.

Source: < www.oiep.bia.edu> Bureau of Indian Education website.

The Reorganization Act's intention to give Tribes greater autonomy and control over their youth's education was not enforced in Segregated Florida.

Tribal Education Timeline

1870: Early Mission Schools

1879: November 1, Carlisle, Pennsylvania, opening of Carlisle School

1884: 200 Indian Schools in operation

1887: 10,000 Indian children in boarding schools

1890: 104 Reservation Day schools

1894: 77 Reservation boarding schools

1896: Congress cut 80% of funds to the Indian Schools

1900: Government funding stopped for church-run Indian schools

Mid 1950s: government schools closed. Indian students to be assimilated in public schools

By 1980 most of the original boarding schools were closed.

Sit In

Ten days after my friends left Florida on the yellow school bus I was back in Mrs. Hunt's class. I adored her as a teacher. I loved school. But, I had to honor my resolution and my friends. Beginning on the first day of school I sat at my desk in silence, hands folded. When I was called on to answer a question I held my silence. When the other students went to recess, I went to the bathroom then returned to my desk, in silence. I spoke to no one. I did not open a book or write a word. Later while the other students were outside Mrs. Hunt stood over my desk, looked me square in the eyes and spoke. "What is wrong? You're my best student and you aren't participating."

"I can't," I said.

"Why not?" She spoke softly. I could hear disappointment, not anger in her voice.

Tears flowed down my cheeks. I began to sob. "The Seminole kids are shipped to North Carolina. They have to leave their parents and they can't go to school with me."

Shock covered Mrs. Hunt's face.

"Who on earth told you that? They stopped doing that years ago!"

"Yes, they do! Ask my Mother!"

My teacher left the room to call my mother. When she returned she pulled me into her arms and promised to find a way to help the Seminole kids. My sit-in was over.

Mrs. Hunt with Butch and me at our 6th grade graduation

With my mother's confirmation of my story Mrs. Hunt called her retired teacher friends. She kept me up to date as her friends worked to help the Seminole children attend public school. One morning she told me the teachers talked to the Elders and families on the reservation. "The parents do want their children to attend school near home." Mrs. Hunt reassured me that the children would go to public school.

Would the Seminole Children Attend Black or White Schools?

One of the major issues to be resolved was determining race. This was segregated Florida. Were the Seminoles to be considered black or white.

Years earlier Betty Mae Jumper wanted to go to public school. She told her story at the 2001 Tribal Incentive Awards and Banquet.

Betty Mae Jumper was one of the first Tribal members to leave Florida to attend school. She told how her interest to attend public school started. Alexandra Frank reported, "She would go to the vegetable fields her mother worked in and saw two young black girls she played with get on a bus to go to school. She asked her mother to see if she could go to school as well. They tried the white public school superintendent first but he said Betty Mae wasn't white so she could not attend any schools there. They next asked the woman whose daughters went to school if she could help. The woman took them to see the principal of the all black school but he told them no because Betty Mae was not black."

Published, September 12, 2001 "Seminole Tribune," written by Alexandra Frank.

Betty Mae was disappointed, then gradually began to believe she would not find a school that would take her. One day, a few months later, she talked to the Agency Superintendent about her dream. He told her the Cherokee Indian School in North Carolina would accept Seminole children from Florida and made arrangements for her to go.

Betty Mae 15, her brother Howard 12, and Mary Parker 14 made that long trip to Cherokee, North Carolina, January 1938 in a Chevrolet sedan used by the government office.

Credit: *A Seminole Legend, The Life of Betty Mae Tiger Jumper*

Separation from their families and the reservation was such a huge change for the three youth, Betty Mae said, "all three of us cried for about a year."

Many other Seminole youth from Florida traveled to North Carolina in the years that followed and continued through the mid 1940's.

Betty Mae graduated Cherokee Indian School then continued

her education in nurse's training at Carbine Indian Hospital. She returned to Florida, serving as a nurse for 17 years, encouraging preventive immunization and safe birthing practices. She is credited with setting up the Seminole Health program.

Stranahan and Abbey Take on the Public School Challenge

Ivy Stranahan, the retired teacher contacted by my teacher, Mrs. Hunt, led members of the Friends of the Seminoles and Daughters of the American Revolution (DAR) to help the Seminole children enter white public school. The Friends of the Seminoles was a committee of the Florida Federation of Women's Clubs. Mrs. O.H. Abbey usually accompanied Ivy Stranahan. These women were determined the children should go to a white public school. They were now faced with the same question the Seminole families met in earlier attempts to send their children to public school. Would the Broward County School District allow these indigenous children in an all white public school?

The description of the Seminole children entering Dania Elementary School is recorded in the DAR article published, May 1962, "Daughters of the American Revolution Magazine." In her article, Mrs. Milo Winters describes the events.

There is a discrepancy between the dates in this article and the recorded entries for Dania Elementary School. All data points to Myron Ashmore as the principal who first accepted Seminole children into his school. He was principal of Dania Elementary only two school years 1947-48 and 1948-49. Tracking the history was hampered by the loss of records Betty Mae Jumper collected and stored in her home. All were lost when her home burned. The fact that everyone remembered the event from their own perspective made the hunt for facts very interesting.

Even Betty Mae had difficulty remembering exactly when the Seminole youth entered public school in Florida. During her June 28, 1999 interview led by R. Howard, Sem 243, she generalized. ...*they stopped going to [Cherokee Indian] school in forty four or forty seven... some where around there. Started to go to public school – opened. The DAR and Friends of the Seminole fight to have the door opened for the Indian kids to go to Hollywood. I mean, Dania.*

What is important, and all agree, is the fact that educating the youth prepared the way for the future advancement of the Tribe.

Education and Progress of the Florida Seminoles

By Mrs. Milo Winters   **A portion of the article follows.**

The formal public school education of the Seminole children began in 1946, when a DAR member was instrumental in getting permission from the Broward County School Board for them to enter the elementary school at Dania, Florida. One of the girls who attended the Cherokee Indian School, knew it was better for children to start school at the age of 6 near home. She convinced the older Indians they should not keep the children home until they were old enough to travel to Cherokee; rather they should be allowed to attend public school here. Thus three Seminole children, who ranged in age from 7 to 10 years old, entered the first and second grades that year. In 1947 seven more children who were 7 and 8 years old, were entered. In 1948 the principal at Dania Elementary School told the Seminole Indians it was necessary to start a kindergarten. The children coming into the first grade the following year needed to learn the Pledge of Allegiance to the Flag, the Lord's Prayer, and answers, in English, to a few simple questions. Two young Seminole girls who had been to the Cherokee Indian School started the kindergarten. Later it was taken over and is still run successfully, by the Baptist missionary's wife daily from 8:30 to noon, September through May. A program and graduation exercise for those who will be entering First Grade in the fall are held at the close of the term.

Broward County Public Schools were the first in Florida to accept Seminole Indians. Seeing that it was good for their children, the Seminoles, in turn, accepted the white man's school. Soon after other schools in Florida received the Seminoles in their area as students. After all, didn't the law state that 'all citizens of the United States of America between the ages of 6 and 16 were required to attend school?' There could be no doubt that they were citizens!

Citizenship for Native Americans

Mrs. Milo Winters statement regarding the Seminole children being citizens was confirmed by the Indian Citizenship Act of 1924, also known as the Snyder Act. This act was proposed by Representative Homer P. Snyder (R) of New York. When signed into law on June 2, 1924 by President Calvin Coolidge, it granted full U.S. citizenship to America's indigenous peoples, called "Indians" in this Act.

1924 Indian Citizenship Act (43 U.S. Stats. At Large, Ch. 233, p. 253 (1924)) reads as follows:

BE IT ENACTED by the Senate and house of Representatives of the United States of America in Congress assembled, That all non citizen Indians born within the territorial limits of the United States be, and they are hereby, declared to be citizens of the United States: Provided That the granting of such citizenship shall not in any manner impair or otherwise affect the right of any Indian to tribal or other property."

Approved, June 2, 1924. [H. R. 6355.] [Public, No. 175.]

Search for Documents Describing First Seminole Public School Education

No records could be found in Broward County School District archives, in the DAR files or The Friends of the Seminoles records regarding the women speaking to the Broward County School Board. No newspaper accounts of this historic event could be found.

Based on all the interviews and other documents available, I believe the following scenario more than likely occurred.

Shortly after my teacher, Mrs. Hunt, called her friend, Mrs. Stranahan, Mrs Stranahan and Mrs. Abbey visited the families and elders on the Dania Reservation. This visit confirmed the parents wanted their children in local schools. Rather than trying to fight with the school board they chose to go directly to Broward County Schools Superintendent, Ulric J. Bennett.(Superintendent 1932-1952) During this meeting they told Bennett to allow the Seminole children to attend Dania Elementary School, a white public school.

Bennett brought up the citizenship question. Stranahan and Abbey showed him a copy of the Indian Citizenship Act. Knowing he could not deny the children access to public schools based on citizenship, he in turn called Myron Ashmore, Dania Elementary School's principal. (Dania Elementary School Principal 1947-1949, Superintendent 1961-1968). Stranahan and Abbey witnessed this call.

These two women were well known and experienced in creating change. Once it was established that the Seminole parents truly wanted their children to go to public schools close to home, and that they were citizens, the entrance into the local school system took place quickly and quietly, with no fan fare, or publicity.

I am still hopeful that documents will be found recording the historic event. This remarkable milestone took place at least eight years before the beginning of the National Campaign to desegregate schools.

That fall of 1947 three Seminole children were selected to attend Dania Elementary School in Dania, Florida. My teacher told me the Seminole children would now be permitted to attend public schools. My dream for my friends was coming true.

The actions by Stranahan and Abbey, described above, was a culmination of many attempts to provide education for the Seminole children on the Dania Reservation.

An interview with Betty Mae Jumper, conducted by Janette Cypress for the University of Florida Oral History Program alludes to the Federal Government's attempts to start an early education program for the Dania reservation children. Cypress asked Betty Mae, "So, there was a school here in Dania for the Indian kids." Betty Mae reported the teacher, *Mrs. Deball ran the school for a little bit. Tried to teach but hardly anybody go to school there.*

Credit: University of Florida Oral History Program.

1930 Dania Reservation Education Attempts by the Federal Government

Young Seminoles with their teacher at the Dania Indian Reservation, Florida. Circa 1930.
Names listed: Betty May Tiger, Mary Parker, Agnes Parker, Howard Parker, Moses Hill and Mary Tommy

Credit: State Archives of Florida, Florida Memory, http://floridamemory.com/items/show/44513

1940s Government School on Dania Reservation

Charlotte Tommie Osceola in an interview with Virginia Mitchell, reported a school house was located next to the agency house where she went for her early education. She named her classmates in the little school as: Betty Mae Tiger, Agnes Bowers, Jack Osceola and Mary Bowers.

Credit: University of Florida Oral History Program.

[This school was closed before Mrs Stranahan and Mrs. Abbey started a day school, in 1943, to prepare the children to go to Cherokee Indian School.]

Charlotte and Mary traveled to Cherokee Indian School for 6th grade (1947) Then returned after one year.

Credit: University of Florida Oral History Program.

Dr. Myron Ashmore Describes the First Children in Class at Dania Elementary School

Ashmore was principal of Dania Elementary School for school years 1947-48 and 1948-49. He was also my High School principal. I entered South Broward High School September 1949 as an 8th grade student, the first year the school was open.

The following is Dr. Ashmore's 1969 interview. During this interview he recounted how those first students came to his elementary school.

As I recall it, they came as the result of the work of a group of interested people who were known as the Friends of the Seminoles. And Mrs. Ivy Stranahan, who was the first public school teacher in Fort Lauderdale, was one of the leaders in this movement. In reality, I had very little to do with their attending school. They dealt with the superintendent, and I was asked if I objected to taking any of the Seminoles into the public school system, and I said, no, I'd be most happy to have them.

Bringing the Seminole children into the public school setting presented unique problems for the staff and the Seminole children. Prior to attending school these children did not have access to running water, indoor plumbing and walls that restricted them. Dr. Ashmore remembered very well how the Indian children reacted to being in the classroom.

We'd be putting it mildly if we said that they were still a little Wild. They were a little bit clannish and they were not used to being restricted by the four walls of the classroom. They had very little knowledge of, or use of the rest room facilities and things of this sort. So we had some rough moments in the beginning. I think it was through patience of the teachers really, that they started to adjust in the classroom and make proper use of the rest room facilities and things of that sort. I think one of the things that we were most conscious of at that particular time was the fact that, if we were going to make them feel welcome in the school, we couldn't do it by punishing them for things that were really no fault of their own. They were not used to these things on the reservation, and they had to learn to use them while they were attending school.

Most of them could speak English. You really didn't know how much they could speak. They could understand a lot more then they would let you know they could understand. But they could communicate well enough to get along in school. The problem was to get them to talk. They were very, very, shy. . . You'll find the little Indians back then, would be three or four paired off together, they'd talk with each other without hesitation. But when they were around, or a part of a group of youngsters of other nationalities, why, they found it a little difficult to communicate.

They were quite good in the physical education activities. They were great runners and jumpers. It was in this area they seemed to adjust best.

The students accepted them quite well. I think you will find in the elementary grades that this is never a problem. The youngsters seem to accept each other just for what he is. . . As far as I was concerned, I don't believe they really knew there was much difference.

(May 12, 1969 Dr. Myron Ashmore interview by Don Pullease and Barbara Mann as part of the Southeastern Indian Oral History Project, University of Florida, in cooperation with the Seminole Tribe of Florida.)

First Dania Reservation Seminole Kindergarten

In 1948, as a result of the difficult adjustments experienced by those first students Principal Ashmore requested the Seminoles to start a Kindergarten to help prepare their children for the reality of the classroom and being inside a building with plumbing and bathrooms. Laura Mae Jumper (Osceola) and one of her classmates from Cherokee Indian School helped get that first Tribal kindergarten started.

Laura Mae with the children
Edna Siniff (DeHass) photo

56

Mrs. Stranahan Remembers the First Day

According to Mrs. Stranahan's memory of the first Public School day, the children were divided into two groups. She took one group and Mrs. Abbey took the other. Based on the DAR article there were 3 children on that first day. Two first graders and one-second grade student. The following year there were seven.

After the children learned they were going to Dania Elementary School their parents took them to Ivy Stranahan to get school clothes.

In a 1970 interview Mrs. Frank (Ivy) Stranahan explained that the children were brought to her for clothing appropriate to wear to public schools.

They got everything they wanted. I didn't know whether they were going to let me have them or not because I was worried for fear that they might lose their clothes. I said, "Now you let me take these clothes home with me, and on the day for registration, I'll come out there and get you and we will go to the school and register there for going to public school. And that's the way we did it.

(October 25, 1970, Page 30, University of Florida Digital Collections, George A Smathers Libraries. Samuel Proctor Oral History Program,

Mrs. Erma Abbey Remembers Joining Ivy Stranahan

Mrs. Erma Abbey reported memories of her beginnings with Ivy Stranahan in 1973 as she was interviewed by Tom King at her home. Her answers started with her first meeting with Stranahan in 1936.

Mrs. Abbey asked Mrs. Stranahan what she needed. She said, "*Well we have a request from Betty Mae Jumper that she had a student friend in Cherokee she'd like to bring her down here to start the little children on an education program, I said, "Well, what do you need to bring her downs?*

"She said, "We need a hundred dollars,"

"And I said, "I'll see if I can get it for you. I think the year was 1936."

"I went to the state conference of the Daughters of the American Revolution that year as a delegate, and I brought home a check for a hundred dollars, which they said they would give to us. That was the starting of the program, due to the Daughters of the American Revolution. That summer, Betty Mae brought this girl from Cherokee home with her,

and they started—Martha Fewel, Peggy Fewel, Pauline Jumper, Mary's sister Mary Louise, and the little boys around here—in a program to use knives and forks and spoons. We furnished up a little house that was on the reservation with furniture and a stove they could cook on. I went out one day and Martha was taking a bath in the tub under a pump and she said, "Mrs. Abbey, see me take a shower?" And she dumped a basin of water over her head. They learned to keep clean and sleep between sheets and eat at the table. That was really the start. The next years some of the little ones, Martha and Peggy, went to Cherokee to school. ... "

1946 from Mrs. Abbey's memory

"I wanted them to go to school, when they were six years old. That is why I fought with the superintendent and the principal of the school in Dania, for education for six-year-olds. We finally got it in 1946. The children going to school mixed very well with the white children. The principal only gave them a year's probation, but the white children learned so much from the Indian children; they mixed right in and played with them. The first and second grade teachers were so good to go along—my only trouble was with the principal. I shouldn't say his name, but they're head of the Broward County Schools at the present time."

"As they went into the upper grades, some of the children dropped out, but some graduated from McArthur School. Judy Billy and Priscilla Doctor were the two that graduated first from McArthur School."

The interviewer wanted Abbey to go into detail on the opposition from the school administrators.

"Well, they didn't want the children in the schools because they weren't citizens of the United States. I told the superintendent that they were citizens and they'd been made citizens (Citizenship Act of 1924). All the tribes in the United States, In July 1924 by treaty, I supposed from the United States, and he didn't believe it. I thought it was funny that a superintendent of schools wouldn't know that they were citizens, and I think that they evidently found it out a little later. Within three weeks from my first starting to talk to them about putting the children into school, they decided to take them on probation for a year."

Interviewer: Tom King 19 October 1973, In Abbey's home, Fort Lauderdale as part of the Southeastern Indian Oral History Project, University of Florida, In cooperation with the Seminole Tribe of Florida

Remarkable Achievement with No Publicity

Missing in recorded history of that era is the fact that very segregated Florida residents and educators of the Dania Elementary School accepted Seminole children into the White Public School System several years before desegregation became a national issue. Principal Myron Ashmore and the teachers of Dania Elementary School along with the parents and children of the Dania Reservation were courageous and determined to provide public school education for the Seminole children. According to Myron Ashmore, "the children proved to be good students."

The successful entry into public school for those first Dania Reservation children made it possible for all the Seminole children to eventually be accepted into Florida's public schools.

Records show that many went on to college and came back to help their people. These early graduates are recognized as beginning the progressive changes that moved the Seminole Indians of Florida from adverse poverty to the successful business and education machine that drives the Seminole Tribes of Florida, Inc. today.

The Ceremony

Within a month of my sit-in, the first children entered Dania Elementary School. The families living on the Dania Reservation were so grateful they planned an honoring ceremony for me.

The event took place early winter following my refusal to learn because my friends had been shipped to North Carolina, the Elders and families at the Dania Reservation participated in this ceremony. It was their way of saying thank you for bringing attention to their children and their desire to have them attend public schools close to home. I cared deeply for my friends and respected their families.

I learned that even a child can make a difference.

The Meeting Chickee on the Dania Reservation

Edna Siniff (DeHass) photo

Mother's mood was quiet and reserved on that cool winter night as we drove the few miles from our home in Pinewood Park, north of Miami, to the reservation. We had been invited to a very special ceremony.

Before we left home Mother made me promise to keep this ceremony secret. She told me I could not tell anyone. I knew this was serious business, but I wanted to know more. I was excited and full of questions but, unsure what was expected of me.

We met at the old meeting chickee. This was a large semi-enclosed building, an open meeting chickee on the Dania Reservation. Walls were only four feet high. A thatch roof covered the approximately 20 x 40 foot meeting area. Electric light bulbs hung in a few places. All the bare wooden benches were filled with people dressed in their best regalia. They were singing in Miccosukee when we arrived.

Mother and my brother sat on benches at the front of the meeting room. I was ushered to the rear of the room. Dad was not present.

The Elders and other tribal officials sat on a raised platform at the front. The story about my reaction to the children leaving on the bus was repeated for all to hear.

Inside the semi-enclosed meeting chickee on the Dania Reservation. This is a group of young people singing. They often sat with boys and girls grouped on either side of the room. Circa: 1948

Edna, Mrs. W.D.DeHass photo

I sat in the back of the room with a group of women who cared for me. The meeting went on for a very long time. I was sleepy so Laura Mae and her mother had me lie down on the floor, with all the sleeping Seminole children. We lay on newspaper with newspapers placed over us to keep us warm. I fell asleep so have no memory of the first part of the ceremony.

As the time approached for me to be honored the women woke me, wiped my face with a damp cloth and began dressing me in a beautiful, full-length, traditional woman's dress.

The skirt, with intricate designs, was topped by a white, purple-yoked, cape that rested on my shoulders. As the women wrapped the skirt around my small frame I asked why it was so big. The oldest woman in the group, spoke in Miccosukee. She explained the meaning of the clothing. "This is your ceremonial dress for the rest of your life." Her daughter Laura Mae repeated her words in English so I would be sure to understand. I was thrilled. I had a dress I would be proud to wear. I understood then why an adult sized dress was made for an eleven-year-old. Laura Mae's mother, Katie made this beautiful dress.

My head was filled with questions. Out of respect for the ceremony I did not speak very much. As Katie Jumper and Laura Mae prepared me to go to the front of the room I asked softly, "Why am I here?"

"You are being adopted into the Sycamore Tribe tonight," came the answer, just as softly. I did not learn the name they had given me. I understood my ceremonial dress would be with me as long as I lived.

After the ceremony I felt a kinship with all Native Americans. That feeling is even stronger today.

I am standing next to Laura Mae. Then my Mother, Edna DeHss. Laura Mae's mother, Katie Jumper, is in front of my brother Butch. Moses, Laura Mae's brother is on the end. Moses was one of the Elders who led the ceremony.
Circa 1948 W.D. DeHass photo

The Meaning of the Ceremony

As an adult, while spending time with an Ojibwe Elder in Minnesota, I asked if he knew anything about the Sycamore Tribe. His eyebrows raised as he asked, "How do you know about the Sycamore Tribe?" When I told him I had been adopted into that tribe by Seminole Elders, air passed quickly through his lips. He looked at me more intently, then smiled broadly. I was intrigued by his reaction and asked him to tell me more. His answer surprised me.

"That is the highest honor any tribe can bestow on a white person. You must have done something really special."

I told him my story.

I knew I had received a great honor at the time. Now I wished I had been brave enough to ask more questions at the ceremony.

I wonder often, why my parents were so frightened for me to be part of the Seminole people. Hadn't they given up their quiet life to aid a people who had been persecuted by our government for nearly 200 years? Then, why did they fear for me to have knowledge of the ceremony that has had such an impact on my life?

Years later Mother told me, "In 'white' Florida there were people who might have killed you for being *too* close to the Seminoles."

The Ceremony Dress.
Edna Siniff (DeHass) photo

Charlotte and me eating at Laura Mae's wedding dinner. The Meeting Chickee is in the background.
W.D. DeHass photo

Education on Brighton Reservation

Children on the Brighton Reservation had a totally different education experience from those at Dania.

September 13, 1938 was the beginning for education on the Brighton Reservation. This was the day Mr. and Mrs. William D. Boehmer arrived. Mr. Boehmer was hired by the Federal Government as the teacher in the newly constructed one-room school. Their living quarters were attached to the school. Boehmer continued as its teacher until the school closed in 1954.

Reference: William D. Boehmer interview. Southeastern Indian Oral History Project, University of Florida, in cooperation with the Seminole Tribe of Florida. February 23, 1971.

Alice Micco Snow wrote her account of education on Brighton Reservation. Reprinted with permission of the University Press of Florida.

In 1939, Mr. and Mrs. William D. Boehmer, two white teachers hired by the federal government, established a country day school on the Brighton Reservation. A bus would visit the scattered camps to bring the children to school. The student population outgrew the school in 1954. Children were transferred to local Glades County Schools. During these years before the integration of local county schools, Indian students were assigned to local, mostly black schools. The Seminoles soon realized that the education in those schools was inferior and refused to send their children. After fighting to attend their county's white schools, the Seminoles came to believe that those schools too, discriminated against Indian children. As a result, the Tribe contracted to send their children to schools in the adjacent county. This worked well until the home county administration learned they would receive federal funds for each Indian child and sought to re-enroll them. The Brighton residents would have no part of this switch. When the home county threatened to prohibit Okeechobee County school buses from crossing Glades County lines to pick up Indian students, the tribe quickly purchased its own school buses to transport the children to the selected schools.

These actions and increased education in public schools indicate how important education is to the Seminoles. Many residents have finished high school while others have college educations and advanced degrees.

Reference: "Healing Plants, Medicine of the Florida Seminole Indians," in the section on Education.

The distance the students had to travel to Okeechobee County and Glades County schools was almost the same. Glades County Schools wanted the $800 per student Impact Aid money the Federal Bureau of Indian Affairs pays a school district for educating each Indian student. Okeechobee wanted the Seminoles to pay a $180 out of district fee, per student, per year. Because the families believed the Okeechobee schools were better for their youth they fought for their choice.

Reference: "Indians Ignore Decision, Schools focus of dispute." Palm Beach Post, July 12, 1980, By Ken McKinnon, Post Staff Writer.

The disagreement between the Brighton families and the Glades County School Board continued until 1988 when Betty Castor, the Florida State Education Commissioner, ruled that Seminole children can leave the reservation to attend school in a different county.

Reference: Hallifax, Jackie. Indian Children to Attend Public School of Choice, Official Rules. Associated Press Archive. August 19, 1988

Determination by the Brighton families to provide quality education for their children resulted in the creation and construction of Pemayetv Emahakv, the first Seminole charter school. Pemayetv Emahakv translates to "Our Way." This school serves students grade K-8.

The Pemayetv Emahakv Charter School (pema-YA-ta ema-HAG-ah) was the brainchild of the Seminole Tribe's Education Director Louise Gopher, the first Brighton Seminole woman to graduate from college. She has been a leader in the cause for education and remains a credible and respected liaison between the Seminole reservations and the Anglo world. The Brighton Reservation Charter School opened in August of 2007 with 146 students, and the attendance has increased each new school year.

Source: April Cone Van Camp, B.A. Doctorate dissertation, College of Arts and Humanities, University of Central Florida, 2008

School Mission Statement

Pemayetv Emahakv Charter School exists to provide parents, students and the community of Brighton with a school that meets high standards of student academic achievement by providing a rigorous student oriented curriculum, infused with the Seminole Language and Seminole Culture, in an environment that is safe, nurturing, conducive to learning and designed to preserve Seminole traditions.

Source: Sherri Ackerman, redefinED. September 23, 2003. https://www.facebook.com/redefinedonline

Native American Education Records

Early in the Native American education process agents of the Bureau of Indian Affairs, on each reservation, were required to maintain records of the students attending school. School census records were to include names of school-age children, their age, place of birth, and, in some cases, the name of their parent or guardian.

According to records in the National Archives, reports were sent by the agents to the Commissioner of Indian Affairs regarding the enrollment of students from their reservation.

The schools themselves were to maintain individual pupil files, as well as attendance records, and other records of the health of the students, teachers at the schools, etc.

Today, the Indian Agency records are located in the National Archives and at Records Administration system. Some Agency records have been acquired by historical societies or universities.

I was unable to locate any records from the Agency overseeing the Dania (Hollywood) Reservation.

Moving to the Mission House

October 1948: After many years of renting houses and apartments my parents were finally able to purchase a new home in Hialeah.

Our little Hialeah house.
Edna Siniff (DeHass) photo circa 1948

While we were preparing for Thanksgiving in our new house Mother and Dad were asked to serve as the Southern Baptist Missionaries on the Dania Reservation.

A new missionary was necessary because the Southern Baptist Mission Board found themselves in an awkward position when the Native American minister holding that position was accused of abuse.

The Mission house we would live in.
Edna Siniff (DeHass) photo 1948

The Seminole Baptist Church on the Dania Reservation Mission.
Edna Siniff (DeHass) photo 1948

Dania Reservation 1948

Mother accepted the appointment as missionary to the Seminole Indians in November, 1948. At that time she believed she was being considered for the permanent position.

Butch and I were attending Hialeah Junior High School.

Dad worked full time at Hector Supply Company in Miami. His income was needed for our family to survive. His hours were long and sometimes he put a cot in his office and slept there.

When Mother and Dad made the decision to accept the invitation on the Dania Mission they also determined that Butch and I would stay at the Hialeah house until the position was finalized.

We used our Christmas vacation to move Mother to the mission house. Butch and I stayed with her those first few days.

Living on the reservation changed everything I had known. The Mission House was a small, two bedroom, reinforced, concrete-block building. It sat about 50 yards from the Mission Church, located on the Dania Reservation.

Mother, a white woman, accepted the position because she believed she could help the families living under conditions of extreme deprivation. Mother knew her appointment was under scrutiny and believed her performance would give her the permanent position.

My brother, and I continued to attend Hialeah Junior High School through to the end of the school year. We would move to the mission full time when mother believed her position would be secure.

It was the busy season at Hector's. Dad, as manager, often stayed there on nights the plant was running 24 hours per day.

First Night in the Mission House

Dad was not with us this first night. We went to bed early. It had been a long day getting Mother settled. All of us were tired and excited. Butch and I were sleeping at our favorite site, the reservation, where we were close to our friends.

Just as I drifted off to sleep a shrill sound woke me. An underlying thumping sound puzzled my sleepy brain. At first I thought it was an airplane in the distance. Then I realized it was a drum. I looked toward my brother who was in the bed on the other side of the room.

"Yeah, I hear it," He answered my inaudible question.

A shiver ran up my spine as another shrill sound pierced the night air.

"That's made by a human," announced Butch.

We both got out of bed and headed for our mother's room. She was standing at the east window. A full moon flooded the land between the house and the church. A clear sky enhanced the brightness of the moonlight. There was no undergrowth or trees near the house. Shadows in the trees on the far side of the church began to move. They moved into the moonlight when the drumming started up again. We continued to watch. There were three Seminole men wearing traditional men's dress. The shrill sound was coming from a bone whistle one of them carried. The men moved around the house in ceremonial stomp step, drumming, chanting and blowing that whistle. The fear that first gripped me dissipated as the sounds became more musical. We did not panic. We watched the men and began to enjoy the ceremony they seemed to be performing. Their path around the house was at a distance of about 30 feet. The moon was so bright we could see their faces. When they completed three revolutions of the house they turned toward us. We knew they could see us standing close to the window. We did not move until they had gone into the trees on the other side of the church. We wondered what ceremony we had witnessed. Mother told us these men were Elders.

We had not seen these men at any time in the past. We thought, maybe they were protecting us. We didn't know why they came.

We only knew we had witnessed an unusual event. We held hands as mother prayed for the men and for us. She thanked the Lord for sending these messengers.

The next day mother took us back to Hialeah. School would start the next day.

The following weekend these same men came to the mission house door and asked my father to go into the glades with them. He accepted their invitation. Dad had to call Hector's to make arrangements for someone to cover for him. The men returned a few hours later to collect Dad. They were gone nearly a week. When Dad returned we were eager to hear about his trip. All he said was, "Mother, we can't teach these people about God. They can teach us." As time passed we learned Dad had traveled deep into the Everglades in a dug out canoe and that he had great respect for the men who had taken him. They had gone out the Tamiami Trail to a village where dug out canoes were waiting for them. He did not tell us any more about the trip.

Elder Roy Huff and W.D. DeHass. Huff and Ingrahm Billie were two of the elders who took Dad into the glades.
Edna Siniff (DeHass) photo Circa 1948

My father was rough around the edges. I knew he was moved by his experience with the Elders. While he didn't talk about his experiences he showed enormous respect for those men and all the Seminole people. We often wondered what had happened to make him so understanding and respectful.

Alone in Hialeah

My friends were now in North Carolina and my brother and I were in Hialeah. I was in seventh grade, my brother in eighth. We were all separated from our families. At least my brother and I were with our family on weekends.

From January to June Butch and I lived in our new little Hialeah house. It was one of those little square houses on a street where every other little square house looked exactly the same. It was in a post-war housing development created to accommodate returning veterans. We had only been in this CBS (cement block with stucco) house three weeks when Mother received the call to serve the Seminoles.

Dad tried to get out to the reservation every night. He didn't want Mother to be there alone. If the men came back he wanted to be with her. Eventually a routine developed. Dad would pick Butch and I up after school on Friday. We stayed with Mother at the mission until Sunday night when Mother would drive us to Hialeah. Dad would go to the plant right after church on Sunday. Monday, dad would show up with groceries before going to sleep at the mission.

Butch and I stayed in Hialeah during the week because Mother and Dad felt we should not change schools. During the years Dad was in the Navy we had to change schools often. Mother did not know how long she would be the missionary at Dania. She hoped the position would be permanent.

My brother didn't like living in the house without Mother. He complained about my cooking, so accepted an invitation to move in with a school friend two houses from ours. I lived alone, Monday through Friday. Dad checked on us by phone. My parents never knew I was alone because my brother always showed up just before Dad arrived. I didn't want it differently because Butch was messy. He made cleaning and cooking more difficult.

During these months my favorite part of the day was coming home from school and sitting on the back step talking to a large crow that adopted me. Crow sat on a post, marking the edge of our yard, calling to me. When Crow called I brought a piece of hard dry French bread to him. At first he kept his distance. I'd throw a chunk of the hard bread on the ground. He'd pick it up and fly to the birdbath, drop the bread in the water and bounce it with his bill until it was soft enough to eat. Eventually he took the bread from my hand. He was very verbal. We carried on a conversation never knowing what each other was saying, yet enjoying the conversation.

Move to the Reservation

At the end of the school year it appeared Mother would have her position longer than anticipated. Dad rented our house to Maud Strong, an elderly woman friend. Now Butch and I would live on the reservation with Mother full time.

Life on the Mission was good for me. I was happy we had moved away from the busy city. I did not like living in Miami or Hialeah. There were no woods and the other kids did not share my interests. Here on the reservation life moved more peacefully. I could hear the wild birds singing and I was treated with kindness by all of the Seminole people.

One of the first things my parents did as "missionaries" was to travel to the different Seminole reservations to survey the needs of the people. Big Cypress was the first on our list. While there I had a chance to renew my friendship with Josie and Susie Billie.

We drove to Brighton Reservation on the north side of Lake Okeechobee during the Holidays, then out the Tamiami Trail to visit the camps along that highway.

After visiting these sites Mother realized, by comparison to the other Seminole locations, the families on the Dania Reservation were having a very difficult time. The families living in Big Cypress, Brighton, and along the Tamiami Trail had gardens and were able to raise some of their food. They also had access to multiple native foods. These three areas provided food in a way the land on Dania Reservation could not. Hunting for game and gigging fish and frogs provided protein. Cabbage palm and other native plants were abundant at the other locations. By contrast the Dania Reservation was barren.

Dania reservation was on deep, white sand. All the undergrowth had been stripped from the land in the 1920's. Deep-rooted large oak trees provided shade. The soil under them could not sustain any plant growth. Game was depleted. Basically there were no natural, edible foods on the Dania Reservation. The people were hungry.

We traveled to Brighton Reservation in the winter. Benches were carried out of the church to worship in the warming sun.

W.D.DeHass photo

Most of the people bowed their heads in prayer. I was fascinated with the feathers on Santa's hat so took out my little Brownie camera and snapped this photo. I wasn't the only one who sneaked a peak at Santa, who walked in during the prayer. The white "fur" of his beard and suit was cotton batting.

Edna Siniff (DeHass) photo Circa 1948

Mother contacted the Mission Board to let them know the conditions and the needs of the Dania families. They promised a shipment from the warehouse of donated goods.

Mother also called on churches in the Miami and Ft. Lauderdale areas. The church families responded by bringing food and clothing. Mother also reached out to local businesses. Bushels of citrus fruit came from nearby groves. Dented canned goods and cans with no labels came from some of the grocery stores. Products that were still good but could not be sold showed up in the donation boxes. The cans without labels were opened one at a time, as needed. If the contents were identifiable they would be added to a meal.

It was common during this era for labels to come off canned goods in the store. The humidity was usually high and the glues used to attach the labels were water-soluble. This was before air conditioning. Store managers often displayed baskets filled with bare cans. If the customer was willing to take a risk they could be purchased cheaply. Everything from vegetables and sauces to pet food had the same problem and ended up in the same bin.

The first semi load from the mission board arrived with much excitement. As the barrels were unloaded I began to doubt the wisdom of the donors. Some of the fabric of the clothing was lovely, but all the buttons and fasteners were removed. Mother and Laura Mae with a team of Seminole women went through the load carefully, salvaging the useful items and setting aside the things that would be discarded later. The last barrel off the truck was filled with bubble gum. I stood back and looked in awe. Here we were with hungry people, and the semi load was barely usable.

By now our family's reserves had run out. We lived week to week on Dad's salary. I began to wonder what "Christian" meant. Mother carefully mentioned to the churches that useful items were important. She feared making waves would cause the donations to stop altogether. Even though most of each load was not usable, she preferred to keep them coming.

Baptist Mission

Members of the Seminole Baptist Church at Dania Reservation were proud of their faith and their membership.

The church bell summoned people to meetings and in an emergency.
Edna Siniff (DeHass) photo

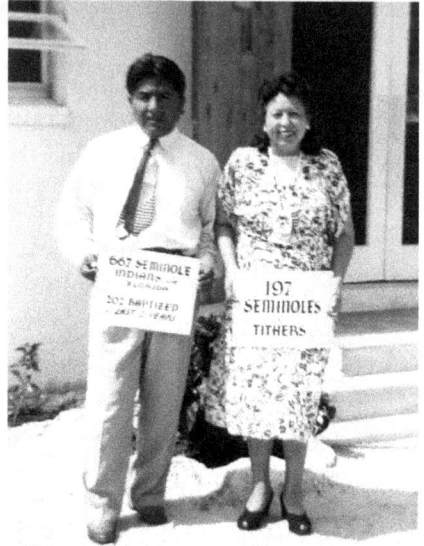

667 Seminole Indians in Florida
202 Baptized in Last 2 years
197 Seminole Tithers
W. D.DeHass photo, Circa 1948

Henry Cypress frequently presented sermons. He often visited the mission.
Edna Siniff (DeHass) photo

The Sunday School Shelter used by all. The first Kindergarten often used this shelter.
Edna Siniff (DeHass) photo

Turkey-Early 1949

Our arrival to the reservation was not an easy transition for the Tribal members, or our family. We were cognizant of the fact that we were the outsiders. For Mother to succeed each family member had to focus on learning the subtleties of the social structure of this community. Basically the do's and the don'ts.

The arrival of a dressed wild turkey made us believe we were accepted by the Elders. To us, the turkey was very special. It felt like we were having a "first Thanksgiving" experience. The effort on the part of the elders to hunt, dress and transport this bird to our home from Big Cypress did not go unnoticed by all of us. We were truly thankful.

The bird arrived one morning while our family was eating breakfast. A knock on our door interrupted our conversation. Three elders, one holding a freshly killed wild turkey, entered our home. These were the same elders who did the stomp dance around the house on our first night. Mother was gracious as she accepted the bird, then headed to the kitchen to cook it in the tradition of our culture. The men stood by while the bird was prepared.

The elders explained that three young hunters were sent into the glades to find the bird. That it had taken days to locate a bird they could shoot. Once in hand, runners passed the bird in the same way as the Olympic torch passes from one runner to another. Moving it quickly to a road where it was driven to our home.

The men watched as the tribal gift to our family took its place of honor on our table. Then stood silently while we ate, refusing to even taste it. A gift of honor could not be shared with the giver, . . .we thought.

While in Florida to continue research for this book, I met Patsy West, Ethnohistorian. Based on her research, she explained the true symbolism of the turkey presented to our family.

"They didn't eat turkey at that time. They probably thought you would die if you ate it." A lively discussion followed this revelation. My thoughts flew back to that wonderful meal and the three elders standing near the table, watching us eat. If they feared eating turkey I wonder what was going through their minds as they watched our family luxuriate in the meal highlighting this flavorful bird. It was the best tasting turkey I have ever eaten.

Walking Food

Late June of the first summer at the mission I learned there was a young horse tied to a tree a short distance from us. The ground around the tree was bare. There was no grass anywhere. It's owner could no longer care for her. I begged my dad to buy her for me. We went to see the horse and the owner. The horse was a young Arabian, very thin, and skittish. The owner said he needed $5 for her. Dad paid the money and the man agreed to bring her to the mission house. There was a large pine tree behind the house. That is where he tied my horse, Sandy. I took a washtub of water to her. As I approached she pawed the ground and snorted. Believing she was afraid of me, I put the water down where she could reach it and moved back to watch. She drank and drank. Big gulps of water swelled her throat as she swallowed. Dad brought feed sweepings home from Hector's Supply that night. We acquired clean hay from a local farmer, a bale at a time. He also let us tie her on his land to graze. Sandy would no longer have to go without food.

Now some of the families began bringing their animals to the mission. They didn't have enough food for the young hogs they carried home from

Me with a piglet from Big Cypress

78

Big Cypress. Some of the men helped us build a hog pen a distance from the house.

The first hogs raised in the new pen.
Edna Siniff (DeHass) photo

A small pond was dug in the sand. The water table in this area was close to the surface. They reached water only two feet down. The sides of the pond were sloped so the hogs could get in and out. The white sand made a wonderful place for hogs. Again, dad brought feed home from Hector's. The Seminole hogs were also fed from the sweepings the workers at the plant collected after filling sacks of feed. Some of the mystery food cans donated by the stores appeared to be pet food. If we couldn't figure out how to add the mystery food to a meal for people we put it in the hog trough.

Hogs grow fast. When the people needed a hog, they came and picked one out. We never knew how many hogs we would feed each day because young ones would be added to the pen and older hogs would be taken away, for food, on a regular basis. Residents on the Dania Reservation now had their own walking food.

Trading Post

One day my brother and I walked to the Trading Post across the highway from the Reservation. We paid a small sum to get in, then joined a crowd of tourists at the wall surrounding the Alligator Pit. There, on the sand by the alligator pool was a young man and his little son. The father had a massive gator, his little boy had a live baby reptile. Everything the father did, the child mimicked. When they finished their performance spectators threw coins into the sand. The father and son crawled around, sifting the sand through their fingers to find the desperately needed money.

The sight of them on hands and knees so close to a pool filled with large alligators turned my stomach. Couldn't they put the money in a jar? Did they have to humiliate the young father like that?

After the spectators left I approached the man, "Why do you have your little boy with you? Aren't you afraid he will get hurt?"

He was very sincere when he answered. "I make sure my boy is a long way from the pool. When he comes with me the people throw more money."

We learned parents would do everything possible to provide for their children. Their children often helped.

Sick People

The calm atmosphere of the mission house ended when an epidemic of pneumonia traveled quickly through the residents on the Dania reservation. Many people were very ill. Malnutrition made them more vulnerable. Rains began to fall. Our little house quickly overflowed with sick people. Pneumonia and malnutrition were driving women with their children and elderly men and women to us. A continuous kettle of sofkee simmered on the stove. Mother tried to get medical help but was told that medical funds for the Seminole had run out.

Our whole family and anyone available nursed the sick. It was difficult to walk through any room because the floor was wall-to-wall people. Food and blankets were in short supply so my parents went begging, again.

At the beginning of this epidemic Laura Mae Jumper began coming daily. She served as interpreter and taught mother how to cook the more common "Indian" foods.

Mother also begged for medical help. Medicine was needed to treat the people who had pneumonia. Laura Mae had contact with the "Healers" and made arrangements to have them come to help. That was when I gained respect for the Seminole Medicine People. They came and camped at our door. Teas were made and given to those in need. The sick received dedicated care.

As the number of sick people increased Laura Mae offered to help mother even more. She found others willing to cook, clean, and take care of the sick. Knowing we were limited by the language barrier Laura Mae brought Frances Tigertail to help us learn Miccosukee. At the time I thought Laura Mae and Frances were adult women. Both were teenagers.

When the epidemic was at its peak Nicodemus and his mother fell against our door. Mother and I ran to them when were heard the thump. As the door opened the mother fell through the door, unconscious, into mothers hands. I caught her baby as he fell from her arms. They were both near death from starvation. I cuddled Nikki while Mom rattled around in the kitchen preparing sustenance for the two. She brought a liquid mixture and a large dropper with instructions for me to drop the fluid on the baby's tongue as often as he swallowed. She held a glass of liquid to his mother's lips. As soon as she had a little liquid in Nikki's mother we carried them to the car. Mom headed for the hospital. The receptionist said there were "No funds," then sent us away. We headed to our family doctor. He could only tell us what to do. Discouraged, we headed home. Over the next few days, we took shifts getting fluids into Nikki and his mother. Nicodemus was so dehydrated he had difficulty swallowing. He slowly slipped away. He died in my arms. The cause of death entered on his death certificate was starvation.

The impact of his death changed my youthful attitude towards the world. How could a baby starve to death in the shadows of large cities like Miami and Fort Lauderdale?

Nikki's Funeral

Nikki's funeral was quickly planned. A small white coffin held his frail body. A deep hole in the white sands of the reservation cemetery was prepared to receive him. Everyone able to walk attended his grave-side funeral. I was given the honor to stand by his mother and throw the first handful of sand on his coffin. I hugged his mother as I sobbed. Our tears mixed on our cheeks.

There wasn't time to grieve for this tiny child. The others continued to need help. Tears came at night when it was time to sleep.

When news of Nikki's death reached the local church community an out-pouring of help flooded the mission.

Some churches prepared whole meals for the Dania Reservation families. They arrived with everything from lemon aide to fried chicken

Lemon aide was a favorite.

Edna, Mrs. W.D.DeHass photos

One of the local dairy farmers, who also milked goats, brought a lactating nanny goat for the babies. The farmer taught me to milk her and cautioned Mother to pasteurize the fresh milk before giving it to the infants. He explained that Nanny, as I called her, was an older goat and would no longer be bred. When she dried up we were to offer her as a meat animal to the families. Over the next several months my morning and evening chores included milking Nanny for the babies. Mom pasteurized the milk, poured it in sterile canning jars and held it in the refrigerator for babies. Runners came for the milk nearly as quickly as it was cooled.

My sister Betty Burden with Nanny and my dog Bonnie.

Edna Siniff (DeHass) photo

83

Visit from the Mission Board

Shortly after Nicodemus died, three men dressed in smartly pressed black suits with white shirts and blue ties came to our home. As I opened the door I told them we had a house full of sick people. The men frowned as they looked at our people covering the floor. Stepping gingerly around the bedding and people, the men headed for the kitchen where Mother was preparing lunch for everyone. I hovered in the shadows near the door, to listen. They introduced themselves then admonished Mother for having all those heathens in this house of God. Many angry words were exchanged. Finally one of the men threatened Mother. "If you don't get these heathens out of this house immediately we will arrange to have you removed from the mission."

Mother slowly lifted the kettle off the hot burner. Rubbing her hands in her apron she looked up at the tall man and said, "for I was hungry, and you gave me meat: I was thirsty, and you gave me drink: I was a stranger, and you took me in: naked, and you clothed me: I was sick, and you visited me: I was in prison, and you came to me. And the Lord spoke: Verily I say unto you, Inasmuch as you have done this unto one of the least of these my brethren, you have done it unto me. (Mathew 25:35-40) I am doing God's work here. These people need help and I will continue to provide help as long as necessary."

She asked where she was supposed to help the sick if not in her home. They told her she was not to help the sick at all, that was work for the medical profession.

Mother was devastated.

As the team left, I asked the tallest, "What does it mean to be a Christian?"

"To convert the heathens to Christianity," came his reply.

I answered, "I don't think Jesus would ignore sick people."

He frowned and said, "You should show more respect for your elders."

I felt he should show more respect for the sick Seminole people.

I held the door open for the men as they left. I was very angry with them because they showed no compassion for our sick people. I couldn't hold back as they passed and blurted out, "who made you God?" A long finger pointed at my face, very close to my nose. It's owner replied, "Little girl, you will go to hell for saying that!"

A big smile crossed my face as I said, "See Ya There!"

Medical Association Clinic building

Hearing the desperate needs of the reservation Seminoles the medical association in the South Florida area raised funds to build a small infirmary. They purchased a World War II barracks building and had it moved to the mission. It was placed a distance to the west of the mission house. Within a short time it was filled with beds and equipment. The doctors organized volunteers to treat the ill. They became our knights in shining armor. We now had a safe place for the sick and knew they would receive care.

This infirmary was not a complete solution to the medical needs of the Seminole people, but it helped. And it certainly brought attention to the human condition of the Tribes.

The new building soon held the people who had been on our floor. Donations of food and clothing continued to come in from the local area relieving the widespread malnutrition. Life for all of us settled into a more normal routine.

The infirmary as it arrived. Some doors and windows were changed.
Edna Siniff (DeHass) photo

Mother's Illness

Not long after the last sick person left the mission house mother became ill. The pain in her legs was so intense she couldn't tolerate weight on them. Her legs swelled to such a degree I feared her skin would split. Laura Mae wet towels, cooled them in the refrigerator then gently laid the cold cloth on Mom's legs. Our family doctor came to see Mother. He had no answer for her condition, or even a name for it. Penicillin had just been discovered so he gave her an injection of the new miracle drug. The drug made no difference.

Word spread through the tribes that mother was ill. That no one knew what to do for her. The message reached the healers. An older man who had come to make medicine for the sick people came to the door with his medicine bundle. He told us he could help Mother if she would let him. I went to Mom, explained his offer, and asked if she wanted him to try to help her. She agreed.

The healer sat on the porch in a comfortable chair Laura Mae brought from the living room. He sang his songs as he made the tea. I watched with great interest. Many different herbs were used. The water was room temperature. When the healer finished he handed the cup to me and told me to give it to Mother, *slowly*.

Laura Mae had Mother sitting in bed when I came in. We held her while she took her first sip. The look on Mom's face and the way she pulled her head back told me it must be really strange. She swallowed, then said, "That's the most bitter thing I've ever tasted." She was reluctant to take a second sip. We chastened her a little. "Nothing else has helped you." Mom agreed and slowly consumed the entire cup. A few hours later the routine was repeated. Mother began to relax. After the second cup she drifted into a deep sleep. When she awoke the pain in her legs was somewhat diminished. Feeling that the tea was helping she eagerly accepted each cup as it arrived. The healer called Mother's illness a word that could be translated to something like "Elephant Leg." Within a week of the healer arriving, Mother was on her feet. She gradually regained her energy.

The August 1949 Hurricane 2

Hurricane season arrived with several Atlantic storms followed on our family's map taped to the dining room wall. The map was published in the Miami Herald at the beginning of each hurricane season. It was in the center of the broad sheet and covered both pages. Cardboard behind the map permitted pins to be pushed into the longitude and latitude lines reported by the radio station. The location was reported daily. Our family followed each storm with great interest.

The intensity of the storm was measured by crews flying specially-equipped aircraft into and over the storms each day. The second hurricane of the 1949 season was especially strong and was headed straight for us. The Weather Bureau had not begun giving hurricanes names. This was Hurricane 2 of 1949.

The center of this powerful storm came on shore near Lake Worth, Florida as a category 4 hurricane with sustained winds of 110 miles per hour. Palm Beach International Airport reported gusts up to 155 miles per hour. The most severe damage occurred in South Florida, Palm Beach, Jupiter and Stuart in particular. Approximately 90 percent of homes and buildings were damaged in Stuart, leaving about 500 people homeless. The tropical cyclone caused $52,000,000 (1949 USD) in damage, most of which was in the state of Florida. It was the costliest storm of the season. It caused the death of two persons and injured 133 others, twelve seriously. The strongest wind occurred, as usual, some distance to the right of the eye in the vicinity of Jupiter and Stuart, Florida. The anemometer failed at Jupiter Lighthouse after reaching a velocity of 153 m. p. h.

December 1949 Weather Review published by the Weather Bureau, Washington, D.C.

Prepare for Hurricane

The mission house was preparation center as this storm tracked across the Atlantic toward us. Dad and Butch covered each window with boards. Dad always left a peephole for us to look out. The church was also boarded up. Blankets and pillows were piled in the living room.

A lantern and the camp cook stove were in the kitchen ready for the power outage. Boxes of nonperishable food filled the space under the dining table.

A large quantity of potable water was needed. The power was usually turned off before the power lines blew down. There was no way of knowing how long we would be without the water pump working. Dad bought WWII water storage containers from the military surplus store. These were filled then stacked against the wall under the window in the dining area. A battery-operated radio was a high priority. Everyone actively participated in survival preparations.

Mother and Dad anticipated many families coming to ride out the storm with us. Their chickees were not a safe place in hurricane force winds. The weather bureau continued reporting the location of the storm. Even when we were in the fury of the winds, we wanted to know where the eye of the hurricane was located.

As the storm approached landfall the Weather man reported dry ice was being dropped into the storm to, hopefully, cool the air and reduce the strength of the winds. We believed it had an opposite affect.

The people on this reservation lived in chickees, a thatched roof open home. They had weathered many hurricanes in the past. Everyone knew what to do. Families helped each other secure their belongings. Each family placed their clothing and other items in the center of the platform on which they lived. Several men worked together to lower the thatched roof to protect the items on the platform and to protect the roof. In many cases the roof thatch touched the ground. The sanctuary and mission house were the safest buildings available. The Agency house would have been a safe shelter also. Families began arriving early in the afternoon. As the storm winds intensified more families and elders joined us in the mission house. Many were also in the church. No one stayed in the new infirmary building.

There were so many people in the house it was hard to find a place to sit. About ten of us were standing in Mother's bedroom facing the east wall when the winds pulled so hard on the house the wall began to lift. It raised the concrete block wall a couple of inches off the cement slab foundation. Water from the pounding rain poured through the opening onto the floor. I thought the wall was going to collapse on us. Everyone in the room with me moved away from the wall. Just as quickly as it had opened, the space between the wall and floor closed.

Mother's bedroom was in this corner of the house.

Edna Siniff (DeHass) photo 1948

The storm was fierce when screams pierced through the roar of the wind. A woman was caught in its fury. The men quickly formed a human chain to hold a rope tied around my father's waist. As they opened the door the wind whipped through the house. The men pushed Dad into the wind and across the screen porch. As he unlatched the screen door, it blew away. The screams stopped. Dad felt around the opening thinking the woman was huddled against the house. Reaching into the pitch-black darkness, brightened only by lightning flashes his searching hands revealed nothing. Now the only sound was the raging storm. "God help us," Dad shouted into the wind. His hand reached above his head. Instantly a piece of fabric slapped his wrist. As he tugged on the fabric the woman's foot brushed his arm. He grabbed her foot. "I've got her," he shouted. A second set of hands caught her other foot. The two men held the woman tight as the group pulled them into the house. They literally pulled the woman from the grasp of the storm.

After she calmed down the woman told us she misjudged how long it would take to walk to the mission house. The swirling wind lifted her off the ground a half-mile from her destination. It could have taken her anywhere. As if guided, it carried her to the mission house. She was frightened but unharmed.

Everyone in the house felt the presence of God and knew we had witnessed a miracle. We all bowed our heads in prayer.

Gradually the storm made its way across Florida. As the winds calmed we began checking the buildings. To our dismay the new infirmary building was flattened by the strong winds. Thankfully no one had taken shelter inside.

Edna Siniff (DeHass) photo

The families who lived in chickees returned to their camps. Missing thatch was replaced when the roofs were lifted back into place.

While confirming the dates and strength of this storm a meteorologist reported "the winds in the 1949 Hurricane 2 were very strong and could have created the lifting of the building or possibly a tornado was nearby. It sounds like you were very lucky," he said. At the time we believed a tornado spawned inside the hurricane caused all the damage around us.

The medical community was not deterred by the loss of their building. They began fund raising to replace it. By the end of the year a new concrete block building was standing firmly on the foundation.

September 1949

At the beginning of the school year two graduates of the new Seminole kindergarten were brought to the mission house each school day morning. I was asked by the elders to check the children to be sure they were ready for school. I was instructed to "make sure they were clean, didn't have lice, have their lessons ready, and they can't miss their ride!" The Friends of the Seminoles provided transportation to Dania Elementary School for these young students. The first little boy I met was Billy Cypress. He was a serious, thoughtful child with a strong desire to learn. There was something special about this little boy. I looked forward to his arrival each school-day morning. He continued his education, from Dania Elementary to Olson Junior High, then graduated with honors from McArthur High School. He was grateful to receive a $2,000 scholarship from the Florida DAR. He also worked many different jobs to pay his tuition at Stetson University.

Following graduation he served in the military, eventually returning to his reservation as a teacher.

By the fall of 1949 the Broward County School Board required Seminole children to provide their own transportation. They could go to public school but could not ride the buses. That rule was still in place when my nieces and nephews entered elementary school in Davie, Florida.

Missing Clothes

My sit-in had a more direct affect on me the day I came home from school to find all my clothes missing. Hanging in place of my dresses, skirts and blouses were two well worn Seminole skirts.

"What happened to my clothes?" I shouted to my mother.

"Laura Mae came by with a few girls who needed clothing for school. She felt they should have clothes like yours. I told her to take what she needed."

As I stared at the two tattered skirts I wished she had left me **one** outfit.

"What am I supposed to wear?"

"The dress you wore today. We'll have to wash it on weekends."

"Geez Mom, the kids at school will make fun of me."

I was in the eighth grade and already shunned by some of the students.

The fact that Laura Mae needed school clothes for teenaged girls meant some of the youth going to school in North Carolina were returning to their homes to attend school in Dania. I couldn't be upset. My dream for the Seminole kids was coming true.

Living in the mission house always had its challenges. Many mixed with the thrill that comes from trusting in God. The day I found my clothes missing ended with one of the churches unexpectedly dropping off a donation box. This was Monday night. The boxes usually came on the weekend. We went through this one immediately. Near the bottom lay a beautiful lavender dress exactly my size. It turned out to be my favorite dress all through my high school years. My wardrobe received new additions from many mission boxes, as did the wardrobes of the Seminole teens.

Laura Mae Jumper and Max Osceola Make History

Laura Mae was at the mission house a great deal. She helped all of us learn the culture of her people. Mother in turn, helped Laura Mae and Max, her future husband, prepare for their wedding including getting their license and medical records. Mother's help made it possible for Laura Mae to have a wedding dress and all the trimmings any bride would cherish. The wedding, held in the Seminole Baptist Church on the Dania Mission made history.

A portion of the article commemorating the event follows.

The Miami Herald, Monday, November 7, 1949

First in History

Two Seminoles Married Under White Man's Law

A Seminole Indian brave Sunday broke a centuries-old tradition by taking a young squaw as his wife in a White man's wedding ceremony. Max Bill Osceola, 20, who was born "somewhere" in the impenetrable Florida Everglades which is his tribe's home, and Laura Mae Jumper, 18, entirely ignored their tribal laws and customs.

Not their tribal chief, but a Baptist minister, Rev. B. T. Beckham of the Pinewood Baptist Church of Miami, led them through the vows that made them man and wife.

From the collection of the Seminole/Miccosukee Photographic Archive. Patsy West

Juanita Fewell served as Laura Mae's maid of honor and her brother Moses Jumper escorted her and gave her hand in marriage to Max Osceola. All the attendents were dressed in beautiful Seminole regalia.

Laura Mae's wedding party after the ceremony. The couple were ready to leave on their honeymoon. Laura Mae and Max are on the right. Brother Moses is behind Laura Mae. Juanita Fewell is next to her. Juanita was possibly the person who helped Laura Mae with the Kindergarten.

Edna, Mrs.W.D.DeHass photo

The church was filled to capacity with the many witnesses to this historic event. Among them were officials from local churches and the Friends of the Seminoles organization.

W.D.DeHass photo

Local churches supplied the dinner served to all in attendance.

Laura Mae and Max acquired one of the small cottages at the entrance to the reservation.

My father, W. D. DeHass, was quoted in local newspaper articles as saying the double ring ceremony was the first Seminole Indian wedding performed in accordance with White man's laws of church and state.

Mother accompanied the couple when they traveled to Dade County Courthouse to obtained their license. Officials there said Laura Mae Jumper and Max Osceola were the first Seminoles to comply with all the provisions of the law, including medical examinations and three-day waiting period.

Cabin that would be the home of Laura Mae and Max Osceola
Edna Siniff (DeHass) photo

Laura Mae (Jumper) Osceola

Laura Mae was driven to help her people. As a teenager I admired her and her ambitions. She was so mature and forward-thinking I couldn't help trying to emulate her. I never saw her dressed casually. She always seemed ready to take on the next challenge.

Annie Tommie and girls
Photo provided by Seminole/Miccosukee Photographic Archive, Fort Lauderdale

Her grandmother was Seminole Annie, Annie Mae Tommie. The traditional camp Annie headed in Fort Lauderdale existed many years before white people settled the city. The people in Annie's camp raised vegetables like corn, potatoes, and pumpkins in their gardens.

During the 1930s Ivy Stranahan drove the men from this camp to the Dania Reservation land to clear it through a WPA project. According to Stranahan, the men were clearing virgin pine forests that were destroyed in the 1926 hurricane. Annie's family members were the first Seminoles moved to the land they had cleared.

When Myron Ashmore, principal of Dania Elementary School, told the elders they had to start a kindergarten, Laura Mae and a classmate from Cherokee Indian School answered the call.

Laura Mae continued to break ground for the Seminole Tribes of Florida. Her life's work is a tribute to the benefit she received from her education and the tenacity she inherited from her ancestors. Her short biography, written by Harry A. Kersey, Jr, appeared in "Native American Women, A Biographical Dictionary." Kersey described Laura Mae Osceola: As a member of the Panther clan who lived most of her life on the Dania Reservation (now Hollywood Reservation). She was one of many Seminole children who attended the Federally run Cherokee Indian School in North Carolina.

Laura Mae and her husband, Max Osceola were the parents of three boys and one daughter. They also adopted James Billie who as an adult was chairman of the Seminole Tribe for 22 years.

The little reservation cabin Max and Laura Mae moved to in 1950 before their baby was born. My mother (Edna DeHass) is holding baby Max.
Laura Mae on right.

Edna Siniff (DeHass) photo

While helping our family on the Mission, Laura Mae talked about her Uncle Sam Tommie who attended Carlisle Indian School during the same years as Jim Thorpe. Laura Mae looked up to her uncles who were respected leaders of the Seminoles long before she was born.

Shortly after our family left the mission Laura Mae found herself in the midst of the struggle to prevent federal termination of the Florida Seminoles as a tribe. Her education and fluency in English and both Seminole languages made her the natural person to be selected as the major interpreter for the older Seminole men during the termination hearings in Washington D.C.. Laura Mae led the fund raising efforts to finance the group's travel to our nation's capital. I was not surprised to learn she was the only woman in the 1954 delegation that saved her tribe from termination.

Kersey described Laura Mae as speaking "forcefully for the elders, effectively answering the pointed questions of the joint Senate-House subcommittee and eloquently presenting the Seminole" point of view and asked for 25 more years to educate and train their people to manage their tribal business and lands. Her effective speaking ability and the presence of the elders caused the bill to be defeated.

In 1957 Laura Mae was selected as the first secretary-treasurer when the Seminole Tribe of Florida was formed. In that capacity she was responsible for setting up the first bookkeeping and office management systems, a position she held for ten years. Her son Max Osceola continued her family's tradition of serving their people.

At age 74 Laura Mae was interviewed by Virginia M. Mitchell. During that conversation she recalled trees and chickees near route 441 and Stirling Roads and her people waiting for the tourist buses to come down the one lane dirt road. Its arrival meant money for their next meal and maybe a treat for the children. Their income came from the sale of their crafts.

She talked about her interest in Tribal Government and her desire to see her Tribe succeed. Her interests led her to participate in meetings under the old oak tree and in the one room clinic.

The old oak tree is the same tree we kids rested under after playing softball. It is now named the Constitution Tree because those meeting under this tree formed the Seminole Tribe of Florida's Constitution.

View from reservation looking through shelters built to sell their crafts along
441. Note sandwich board on road to advertise their "shops."
Edna Siniff (DeHass) photo 1945

Laura Mae explained, "I had a dream that someday we would be self-supporting and that we would not need the government's money."
During her meetings in Washington, D.C. she told the U. S.
Government to continue to recognize her people as a tribe. She told
the joint committee that one day "we will be self-sufficient and we are
determined to see economic development for our people."

Laura Mae wanted to see education for her children and all the
Seminole children so they could be strong leaders in their tribe. In her
mind, education was needed to move the tribe to independence and
self-sufficiency. She believed it was important for their Grandmothers
and Grandfathers to have the care they needed in their older years.

During this interview she said her dream was starting to come true.

"Now that we are seeing progress within our Tribe so that we can
see the day that we will not need their grant money, the government
wants to take away our chance for independence. They want to put us
back where we were, waiting for a bus to make some money 'selling

our arts and crafts.' They gave us reservation land and said 'Here, make the best of what you have.' Now, they want to control what we put on our land so that we cannot use our land to produce income for our people..."

"I love my people and my Tribe. To me, seeing the Tribe become strong is most important. This will assure me that my children's children will be healthy, educated and have a good life."

Laura Mae ended the interview with this statement: "I have seen a lot of things in my lifetime, some good and some bad. However, with the Great Spirit at our side, my dream will become a reality and the best is yet to come!"

Reference: Osceola, Laura Mae, Southeastern Indian Oral History Project University of Florida Interviewer: Billy Cypress. June 24, 1962

Osceola, Laura Mae, interviewer Virgina Mitchell, Seminole Tribe of Florida

View from the chickee nearest the church showing the reservation sand road.

Edna Siniff (DeHass) photo

Time on the Reservation Ends

Life on the Mission settled into a gentler routine after the hurricane season ended and the replacement infirmary was under construction. Memory of the visitors from the mission board was fading. Mother began to think the threat to replace her had passed. Those thoughts were short lived. Late in the fall of 1949 she was told she would be caretaker until a qualified missionary could be recruited. Mother was devastated when she received that message.

Just as the new infirmary building was completed, a registered letter arrived from the Southern Baptist Home Mission Board. The letter Mother received informed her that the permanent replacement for the position of Missionary had been accepted by Genus and Carolyn Crenshaw. After our family left the Mission, Mrs. Crenshaw held the kindergarten classes in the new infirmary building.

Mother served on the Mission at the Dania Reservation from December 1948 to December 1950. There were many mitigating circumstances regarding Mother's dismissal. The primary reason seemed to stem from her admitting sick Seminoles into the mission house. I also believe my brother's intended marriage to Frances Tigertail played a huge role. Many visiting members of area congregations admonished our family. "You can love them but you can't marry them." Segregation seemed to be playing a large role in what our family could and could not do on the mission.

As we packed our things to move we remembered our many experiences living with the Seminoles. The Elders who visited on our first night and how they played an integral role in helping us understand their culture. We took pride in the many accomplishments and progress of the Dania Reservation families. The children were now attending local schools. A small infirmary was providing medical assistance. More children were participating in church activities. Malnutrition no longer played a major role in the people's health. These Seminole families were on the threshhold of major events that would change the future for all the Tribal members.

When Mother was dismissed as missionary our family purchased a farm on Bowers Road in Davie. We used our Christmas vacation to move our family and animals to the Davie farm. Our route carried us west on Stirling road. From the junction of 441 to Davie this road was dirt. The section running east was a two lane paved road that ended in Dania.

My horse Sandy, the goat Nanny, and all the hogs moved with us.

When we left the reservation Nanny no longer gave milk. She was rejected as food and became my pet. Nanny followed me around on the farm and learned to do tricks. When Anthrax ravaged our area of South Florida Nanny and our Morgan horse were infected. Our veterinarian, who came to treat our animals, also became infected. He and Nanny died of Anthrax.

The hogs continued to provide meat for the reservation families, ending only when the people stopped bringing young animals to be raised.

Seminole residents of the Dania Reservation continued to visit us on our farm. A bridge crossing the canal flowing along the east side provided a good platform for gigging. I often hung out with Seminole teens gigging frogs near and on our farm. Frogs provided another food source for the Dania Reservation families.

Frances Tigertail

Frances Tigertail joined the helpers at the mission as a teenager. She grew up in her mother's camp on the Tamiami Trail. Frances was a youngster when her father was killed walking along that highway.

When Frances came to the mission her job was to teach our family Miccosukee. We learned enough to communicate with some of the Elders. Since the language was not written many of the words were fluid. Meaning they were gradually changing between generations.

One day, in the kitchen of the mission house, an elder woman was persistent in making mother understand her request. Machaye she repeated over and over. Finally the woman held up her pointer finger and blew across the tip. AHH! Mother sighed. Matches. Then handed her a box of striking matches.

Another day when Frances was tutoring us a runner came in shouting that a Busgee was coming down the driveway. We were all puzzled. The child had made up the word on the fly. Everyone began using the word when they talked about a bus.

Mother wanted all the women who helped on the mission to be familiar with large grocery stores. She often asked them to buy groceries for the mission. When Frances was asked to go to the store she was frightened. She asked me to go with her. I was in high school so welcomed any chance to go shopping.

As we walked into the store I thought Frances was going to faint. The bright lights, the aisles filled with colorful labels, the smells and the sounds startled her. She sucked in a torrent of air and grabbed my arm so hard she left bruises. I held her shoulders and told her to shut her eyes, then held her until she stopped shaking.

"What's wrong," I asked. Her eyes filled with tears.

"I can't read. I don't know what anything is. I can't read the list your mom gave me. I won't be able to find anything."

"We can fix that," I said.

"How?"

"We'll begin right now. I'll teach you to read."

Frances took Mother's list from her pocket. It was very legible. Mother was proud of her beautiful handwriting.

I pointed to the first thing on the list and told her it was, "Soda Crackers." I held my fingers around the word "Soda" and then around the word "Crackers." We pushed the cart to the aisle displaying crackers.

"You've seen the box of crackers in the kitchen. Do you see a box that looks like it here?" Frances found the box almost immediately.

With a devilish smile on her face she pointed to the words on the box. Then complained, "It doesn't say soda."

"I know, that's what Mom calls them. It actually says Saltine."

By the time we had all the items on mother's list Frances had learned to read many words and knew, generally, the lay of the store. We giggled and laughed on the way home. A few more trips together and Frances was ready to handle shopping on her own.

Frances and my brother took an immediate liking to each other. A romance began to fan between them. I was required to go on every "date." Our parents believed my presence would prevent people from "talking." Having a trio in the car made no difference. Both the white and Seminole communities took issue with Butch and Frances being attracted to each other. The two teens were not deterred. Their love grew stronger. They were determined to honor their love for each other.

Being their chaperone gave me an opportunity to see how the Seminole people were treated in public. Even when Frances wore proper clothing she and Butch were denied entrance into movie theaters, to amusement parks, department stores and public spaces. I usually came into the store separately, keeping my distance, curious about the interaction between employees and Butch and Frances. Store managers or employees would follow them. Many times asking them to leave before they found the item they had come to purchase. Gradually they decided to wear traditional Seminole clothing. They felt strongly that Seminoles should not be denied access to any public stores or spaces.

Dania Beach was one of their favorite places to go. Patrons at this public beach didn't seem to mind the Seminoles. Many of our friends met us at this beach. We didn't have a lot of beach toys so created our own. A great floating device was made by wetting a pillow case then holding the opening toward the wind, fill it with air, squeeze the top close with one hand. Holding the pillowcase balloon with both hands we would throw ourselves on and float toward shore.

Frances surprised me when she asked to ride Sandy. She was in full Seminole dress, yet she nimbly mounted the horse, wrapped her skirt around her legs and took the partially trained filly for a short ride around the mission. Nothing deterred her.

I loved Frances and knew she had an enormous challenge ahead of her. It was truly a collision of cultures–cultures that were so diversely different it is a wonder she survived. How do you care for a house when you have never lived in one? How do you cook on an electric stove when all you have known is an open fire and heavy iron kettles?

A Bi-Racial Marriage

Frances Tigertail and my brother Butch, William Delbert DeHass II, were married shortly after we moved to the farm. The elders were opposed to the union and threatened my brother with death if he didn't treat her well. Frances also brought her son, Joe Don Billie, to live with us.

(No photos were taken of this wedding ceremony. Nancy Larkin, her father and I were the only persons in the yard observing the wedding. The landing the wedding party stood on was very small. Mother and Dad stood in the house at the open door. Rev. Beckham from Pinewood Park Baptist Church officiated.

This sketch was created from Nancy and my collective memories.

After the wedding ceremony my brother wanted to take his new bride to an elegant restaurant on Miami Beach. He asked me to go along.

"Why?" I asked.

106

"Because you know how to talk to people."

I was puzzled, but joined them anyway. We were all dressed in our best Seminole attire. When we reached the restaurant I realized why Butch wanted me there. We were blocked as we tried to enter. The smartly dressed doorman told us we could not enter. "If you want to be served you will have to go to the back door of the restaurant to order. We'll bring your dinners out to you."

I looked at my brother. He was ready to explode. Frances was close to tears. I looked up at the doorman and told him we had no intention of eating at the back door.

On the way home we began planning a way to get into the restaurant. A sit-in was in order. The following Saturday evening three carloads of teen-aged Seminoles, my brother and myself included, arrived at 5:30 to the same elegant restaurant. We did not hesitate when we reached the door. I was at the head of the line, Frances behind me, and Butch behind her. The other four couples fell in line behind us. I walked through the opened door right past the startled doorman. Everyone followed in quick-step formation behind me. We took three tables in different parts of the room. We sat there until 9 p.m. No one served us. Not even a glass of water. Nor did we see a menu. Leaving the table in pairs, we all used the bathrooms. The doorman was now meeting guests and turning them away. Apparently they didn't want anyone to see us in the restaurant. Even though we didn't have an opportunity to eat an elegant meal in a high-end restaurant we felt we had made a statement that Seminole people should be admitted and served. At least we had prevented many wealthy people from eating at that restaurant, that night.

On our way home we stopped at Jumbo Franks, a popular drive-in restaurant that specialized in shrimp. Butch bought a jumbo serving of shrimp and chips for each car.

Looking back on this event, I am amazed, and thankful, the owners of the elegant restaurant didn't call the police to forcefully remove us.

Life for the Seminoles Improves

After we moved to Davie my mother continued to work with those families who desired her help. Mabel Frank, mother of Frances, continued to be close to us. My brother began going to Big Cypress to help with her cattle. Educated younger members of the tribes returned and were involved in structuring the future for the Florida Seminoles. Having protective housing was high on their priority list. The Friends of the Seminoles organization was instrumental in securing financial assistance. Finding ways to provide employment was also necessary.

Housing Changes on the Reservation

Cold weather, blowing rains and lack of sanitation facilities continued to plague the families on the Dania (Hollywood) Reservation. The families desired to have homes like their children's classmates but did not have the funds to build them. The income the men earned as parking lot attendants and alligator wrestlers combined with the income the women earned from sales of Seminole dolls, clothing, and grass baskets as well as working in the tomato and vegetable fields provided the only available income for these families.

"The Seminoles were not able to borrow directly from banks because of a section of the banking law which does not allow banks to loan money for the construction of private residences on government property like the Reservations. Once the Tribe became chartered, loans were administered by the Tribe itself."

Patsy West, Reflections 2, page 2 and 3.

Traditional chickees served as homes for the Seminoles after their villages were burned and they were forced to live in the Everglades. The thatch roof open dwellings served them well when they were built in the thick growth of the Hummocks in Big Cypress and Brighton reservations and along the "Trail." The undergrowth sheltered them from the rain driven by strong winds, making it possible to keep the living area dry. This undergrowth also protected the camp from the cold winter winds as well as providing privacy for the families.

The Dania Reservation presented different challenges for the people living there. It *"had been cleared of underlying vegetation in the 1920's. The chickees were erected under oak trees. ... In the winter, the families were exposed to cold winds which blew across the white sand with nothing to break the onslaught."*

Reflections: Patsy West, At Home on the Res. Article Number 2

Now that the children were attending public schools, they were learning the benefit of running water and plumbing and began asking their parents to consider living in a house with plumbing and electricity. Others on the reservation also wanted to have more substantial homes.

Many barriers prevented them from building houses. Families on the reservation had no collateral and could not receive conventional loans. *"They did not own their land, as it was held in trust by the Federal Government, therefore, they could not get loans from the banks to build houses. That's when the Friends of the Seminoles got creative, coming up with very novel solutions to aid the Florida Seminoles in their housing dilemma."*

Reflections: Patsy West, 2 pp1 and 2

Using newspaper articles and letters to their members, The Friends led a successful campaign to raise funds to help the families living on the reservation.

"We are hoping to find local people who will be willing to back this project," said Friends board member Mrs. B.E. Lawton. *Before the end of the 1950's all the Friends membership fees were designated to the Seminole housing fund.*

Reflections: Patsy West, 2 pp1 and 2

Contributions came from many individuals. The Friends also introduced a plan giving local residents an opportunity to co-sign loans of $850 for Seminole families to build homes. The interest-free loans were to be paid back in ten years at $25 per month. The Ft. Lauderdale National Bank agreed to make all arrangements for the loans and to receive the payments. As the loans were paid the Friends recycled the money making it available for additional families to finance homes.

"Patsy West, Reflections 4 pp2

The reservation became a repository for quality structures that had to be moved due to large construction projects. One of the first moving ventures occurred when the Friends purchased three duplexes from Mooney Point, the future site of the sixteen story Fiesta Towers. The Friends purchased the three for $500. R.D. Bryan, a local contractor agreed to move them, cut them in half, add a bedroom, a porch, electrical wiring, an electric pump and a septic tank for $350.

The first home in the Seminole housing project was that of Henry John and Juanita Billie. Henry John, a parking lot attendant, qualified for the first loan from the Friends of the Seminoles. The Billies visited the house at the beach before it was moved. They would have the distinction of having the first hot water on the Reservation. The Billie's home had a screened in 'Florida room,' two bedrooms, a living room and kitchen.

The next home was for Mary and Joe Bowers.

"Spearheading the movement for modern conveniences on the Hollywood Reservation was the Reverend Bill Osceola of the Independent Baptist Church and his wife Charlotte. Osceola told the Miami Herald, 'Some white men think we still want to live in chickees, but we don't. The Seminoles want to live like everybody else.' He began to build the first CBS (Concrete Block Structure) house on the reservation in 1956. The next year he would be the new Seminole Tribe's first President."

Reflections: Patsy West, Number 3 pp 3.

"The Osceola's savings, private loans, and the Friends of the Seminoles made the Osceola home building project a reality. The Friends guaranteed him a $1,000 loan. … The Osceola home would have three bedrooms, a bath, a kitchen, and dining room. The Reverend spent five months working on the house, which he built himself.

"Other builders worked diligently on less expensive homes. Some were small with only one room and did not have plumbing. Their owners received a $600 loan from the Friends of the Seminoles and felt most fortunate to be a homeowner.

"On November 3, 1956, Alligator wrestler Jackie Willie signed notes with the Friends of he Seminoles to begin construction of his family's interest free, two bedroom home. The Willie family built the fourth CBS house on the Hollywood Reservation. (Formerly Dania Resservation)

"The fifth home was built by Josie Jumper, a 16 x 24 foot CBS home designed for him by Mr. F.D. Sheldon, (husband of Frances Sheldon) a mechanical engineer. Josie had worked for the Dania Indian Agency Office since 1926."

In May of 1958 an offer came to The Friends of the Seminoles that could not be refused. *"Owner of Northway's Marine Villas on Pompano Beach, S.E.. 'Doc' Northway, donated three partially furnished 'beautifully preserved' white frame houses to the building project. The villas, which had been rented to tourist for $200 a week, became the second group of wooden frame houses on the Hollywood reservation."* Source: Patsy West-"Reflections" Historical Series, Seminole Tribune Newspaper Numbers 86, 87, 88, 89 in a series At Home on the Res

Brighton Reservation

On the Brighton Reservation, it was the Florida Federation of Women's Clubs who undertook a special Seminole housing project. The elderly Mrs. T.M. Shackleford from Tampa, a past president of the organization, campaigned vigorously for the funds to build the home of Sally and Reverend Billy Osceola, raising over $2,500, at a time when a door cost $40.00.

Reflections 3 pp3. Source: Patsy West-"Reflections" Historical Series, Seminole Tribune Newspaper. Number 86, 87, 88, 89 in a series At Home on the Res

[Sally and Reverend Billy Osceola on Brighton Reservation and Charlotte and Reverend Bill Osceola on the Dania Reservation are two different families. Osceola is a common name among the Seminole people.]

Alternative Housing on Dania Reservation

Not all the families wanting conventional housing, borrowed money through the Friends of the Seminoles. Mabel Franke and her husband Sam did the next best thing. They enclosed their chickee. The platform was removed and the area between the poles was covered with a raised wooden floor. The kitchen was left open on one side. The bedroom was fully enclosed. My mother co-signed Mabel's contract to purchase a used stove and refrigerator. Mother also signed for the electricity to the remodeled chickee.

Mabel, standing, Frances is seated. Joe Don Billie on table. Bobby facing the new stove and Junior (W.D, III) sitting on the floor.
Photos Credit: Florida Power & Light, Sunshine News Service, February 1956. Author and Photographer unknown.

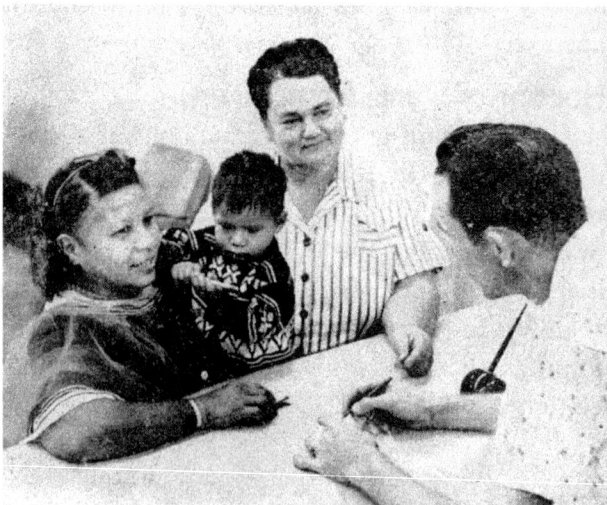

Mabel holding her son with Mrs. W.D. DeHass at signing for electricity.

Power hook up. Frances and sons.   Miss Dorothy Sims and Mabel
Photos Credit:
Florida Power & Light, Sunshine News Service, February 1956.

Spirits were high as the transition to conventional housing began.

Homes with electricity and electric appliances presented many
challenges to the women and to their families. Transition from an
open fire with large iron cookware to an electric range, kitchen sinks
with hot and cold running water, and floors that required sweeping
instead of raking, created new experiences for the homeowners.
Florida Power and Light sent Miss Dorothy Mims, their Senior
Home Services Representative to teach the Seminole homemakers to
use their electric cooking stoves.

As the people on the reservation moved toward comfortable housing
complete with utilities, many persons and groups within the Seminole
and local communities stepped forward. They worked individually
and together to solve the problems these changes presented.

Employment

As housing improved on the Dania Reservation the need for income continued to be a major concern for all the Seminole families.

During the 1950s the Seminole people met the challenge of the Federal Government's attempt to terminate the tribe and used the 25 years they were granted to prepare for the future.

During this same period the people living along the Tamiami Trail determined they should be recognized as a separate tribe. These Miccosukee speakers had spent decades isolated from the reservation families. They had achieved economic independence by developing a tourist trade in their roadside villages.

The Seminole Tribe of Florida was officially recognized in 1957. This tribe included Dania (now Hollywood), Brighton and Big Cypress Reservations. The government built a tourist-attraction village on the Hollywood Reservation.

The separate Miccosukee Tribe of Indians of Florida was recognized in 1962. The Miccosukees received a restaurant, gas station and a school for their "Model Indian Community" on the Tamiami Trail.

The Seminole Tribe experimented with many different ventures to create income for their tribal members. At first they tried leasing some of their land but soon learned it did not generate enough income to support its members. During these early efforts my sister-in-law, Frances, told me she was learning to make telephone parts, possibly in one of the leased land ventures.

The leadership scrimped and saved to send representatives to Washington, D. C. to gain government loans and grants to support their enterprises. The loans were paid back by hosting the first Tribal Rodeo.

In the mid 1970s the Seminole Tribe was suffering a 30% unemployment rate. Many families were surviving on food stamps or other aid programs.

The first economic breakthrough came when the Seminole Tribe created the first Smoke Shop on the Hollywood Reservation. After the initial costs to set up the business, drive through smoke shops sprang up along the highway. The state challenged their right, in court, to sell, tax free, and lost.

Gaming was introduced in the 1960s, but due to religious convictions, the offer was turned down. Under new leadership in the 1970s the tribe began researching high stakes bingo games. The first High Stakes Bingo operation, in the country, opened on the Hollywood Reservation December 1979.

Due to expenses and the partners who owned 40% of the Bingo and a large portion of the Smoke Shop business, revenue left little for the people. The Seminole Tribal members did not see a penny until 1981. The dividend that year was $600 for every man, woman and child.

In 1991 the Seminoles began diversifying their investments. They did not want to be totally dependent on gaming. Among the additional business enterprises was an exotic game preserve. They returned to their agrarian roots with the development of a nursery for landscaping plants, citrus groves, sugarcane fields and, vegetable production. Near the turn of the century they expanded their calf production and Seminole beef became well known, worldwide, for its quality. An additional diversification came with the building of an aircraft company in Fort Pierce.

The desire to provide employment opportunities and income for tribal members and their adaptability to change, opened opportunities for all tribal members.

With the Seminole Tribe's purchase of Hard Rock International, Inc. from the London Based Rank Group, it gained an immediate presence in 45 countries. Hotels and restaurants make up a large share of this recently acquired, established, business.

Today, employment opportunities abound for members of the Seminole Tribe of Florida and the Miccosukee Tribe of Indians of Florida and for thousands of non-tribal members.

The dreams of Laura Mae (Jumper) Osceola are being fulfilled. Not even this forward thinking tribal member could have imagined the financial success the tribes are experiencing today.

Reference: Patsy West, From Hard Times to Hard Rock.

The details of the business and land expansion of the Seminole Tribe of Florida and the Miccosukee Tribe of Indians of Florida is documented by Ethnohistorian Patsy West in a well-researched article, "From Hard Times to Hard Rock." Beginning in the 1930s she reviews the progressive changes leading to their financial success.

Transition From Poverty Ends with Purchase of Hard Rock Cafe

The Seminole Tribe of Florida's purchase of the major international corporation, Hard Rock Café (Hard Rock International, Inc.) gave them an established presence in the Americas, Europe, Asia and Australia.

Tribal Council representative Max Osceola announced this purchase. In his words, "To provide for the tribe, we're looking beyond the border, the four square borders of our reservation. We're looking not just in the United States, but we're looking in the world. So this income will provide for our tribe, for our young people that are coming up."

He was telling us all that his mother's dream for a strong, educated tribe that could provide for itself had indeed come true.

In Florida, The Seminole Tribe of Florida in addition to employing their Tribal members also employs more than 2,000 non-Indians, purchases over $24 million in goods and services from hundreds of Florida vendors every year. Most importantly, the tribe pays over $3.5 million, yearly, in federal payroll taxes.

Going from extreme poverty, threats of termination as a tribe, and their children prevented from a public school education, to achieving financial security happened in only a few decades, basically transforming in one generation. Laura Mae's determination to have a better life for her children and grandchildren was achieved the day her son, Max Osceola, made the Hard Rock Café announcement.

Reflections

Susie Billie

My childhood experiences provided an opportunity to delve into a world hidden from the general population of Florida. I learned, at the shoulder of Susie Billie, a way of life all Seminoles shared. My parents could not have planned this summer experience if they had tried. I wish every child, including the Seminole youth of today, could be in a traditional camp and learn from their elders the gift of life lessons.

While living in Big Cypress I learned the feeling that comes from being shown respect. Susie Billie not only demonstrated the act of respect she also helped me understand the meaning of love. Living in the heart of the Everglades was wonderful. My months in the Billie Camp provided me with a strong foundation that would carry me through all my years. My sorrow is that I was never able to return to Big Cypress, as an adult, to express to Susie and to Josie how much they influenced my life and how much their friendship meant to me. Susie Billie and the time I lived with her and the stories told by Josie Billie are often in my thoughts.

I remember little Nikki and how his death brought attention to the needs of the people on the Dania Reservation. His death impacted my very being and caused me to care about my fellow human beings. I am often visited by the memories of the day he died in my arms. Tears flow for his tiny person when I recall the events of that day.

I am grateful to have met and worked with Laura Mae (Jumper) Osceola. She was an inspiration to all of us. Seeing her determination to change the devastating circumstances she and her people were forced to endure gave me strength to challenge wrong when it came before me.

Laura Mae and Max Osceola's adopted son, James E. Billie, was the mastermind behind the development of the Ah-Tah-Thi-Ki Museum in Big Cypress.

I was excited to see this Museum and to learn Billy L. Cypress had served as the Executive Director. He and James E. Billie had been friends since childhood. Prior to this position Billy Cypress was solely involved in education, utilizing his training as a teacher to help his people. I knew that little boy was special the first time he came to our door.

James E. Billie served 22 years as chairman. During his tenure he was the strong-minded, literal, proponent leading his tribe through economic changes his people so desperately needed.

My high school principal, Myron Ashmore, was very tolerant of my frequent tardiness. We lived beyond the school bus route. I was granted a driver's license at age 15 because I had to drive from our Davie farm to South Broward High School in Hollywood, Florida. The vehicle was a 1936 Ford flatbed farm truck I named Lily Bell. Open range laws were in place during those years. When the water was high the cattle gathered on the dikes that served as my road. Sometimes the cows stood their ground, preferring to argue with my truck for the dry space that soothed their hooves.

Near the end of my Senior year the gas tank fell off "Lily Bell" two miles from school. I coasted to the edge of the road, ran back to collect the tank, then trotted the final miles to school. Myron Ashmore was a little disgruntled. "I've got to see this before I will believe you," he said. He drove me to my truck, crawled under its bed to see where the tank had been. "Where's the tank now?" he asked from beneath the truck. I motioned to it sitting on the truck's flat bed. He whistled. He was very friendly on the drive back to school and was concerned as to how I would get home. I told him my brother would come and tow me home. He wrote an excused tardy slip. No matter the infraction, I always found him fair in his assessment. I know he demonstrated that same patience with the the first Seminole children in his school. I was pleased to learn he was instrumental in starting Nova Schools.

I'm reminded by the struggles of these unique personalities, that no matter the challenge, their efforts provided results that are truly remarkable. I am thankful to have lived a portion of my formative years with them.

Bibliography

Abbey, Erma. Interview. (December 19, 1973). King, Tom. Interviewer. Southeastern Indian Oral History Project, University of Florida. In cooperation with the Seminole Tribe of Florida. (pp. 6).

Ackerman, Sherri. (September 23, 2013). redefinED. Seminole Indian charter School gives students the best of both worlds. Redefined the new definition of public education. Retrieved February 3, 2014. https://www.facebook.com/redefinedonline

Ashmore, Dr. Myron L. (May 12, 1969). Interview. Pullease, Don and Mann, Barbara. Interviewers. Southeastern Indian Oral History Project, University of Florida, in cooperation with the Seminole Tribe of Florida.

Ashmore, Myron. (Feb. 25, 1997) Obituary. Sun Sentenial, I By Bill Hirschman Education Writer

Associated Press Reporter. (July 4, 1988). Children caught in tug-of-War. Lakeland Ledger.

Boehmer, William D. Interview. (February 23 ,1971). Southeastern Indian Oral History Project, University of Florida, in cooperation with the Seminole Tribe of Florida.

Bataille, Gretchen, M. , Laurie Lisa, (2001)(Compilation) Native American Women, a biographical Dictionary" (Biographical Dictionary of Minority Women). Routledge.

Broward County Schools Website. (2015). The history of Broward County Public Schools, Superintendents. Retrieved August 2, 2014. http://bcps.browardschools.com/history/tenure.htm

Bureau of Indian Education website < www.oiep.bia.edu>.

Covington, James W., (1993) The Seminoles of Florida. University Press of Florida.

Florida Seminole Indians.. Gainesville: University Press of Florida, 2001, pp. 20-21.

Frank, Alexandra. (September 28, 2001). Incentive awards and banquet. The Seminole Tribune. (pp. 1, 12).

Give Us twenty-five more years: Florida Seminoles from near termination to self-determination, 1953-1957. Florida Historical Quarterly 68(1989). (pp 290-309).

Hallifax, Jackie. (August 19, 1988). Indian Children to attend public School of choice, official rules. Associated Press Archive.

Hileah pair named to Seminole Mission. Palm Beach Post, Nov 5, 1949.

Kersey, Harry A., Jr. (1996). An assumption of sovereignty social and political transformation among the Florida Seminoles. 1953-1979. University of Nebraska Press. Lincoln.

Kersey, Harry A., Jr. (1974)The friends of the Florida Seminoles society: 1899-1926. Tequesta XXXIV, (pp. 3-20).

Kersey, Harry A., Jr. (January 1978) Seminole Tribal integrity, 1899-1957. Florida Historical Quarterly, LVI, #3. (pp. 297-316).

Kersey, Harry A., Jr., Bannan, Helen. (1995.) Patchwork and politics: the evolving roles of Florida Seminole Women in the twentieth Century. In Negotiators of change: historical perspectives on Native American Woman. Edited by Nancy Shoemaker. (Pp. 183-212). New York. Tourledge.

Knetsch, Joe. Florida's Seminole Wars 1817-1858. Arcadia Published, 2003.

McKinnon, Ken. (July 12, 1980). Indians ignore decision, Schools focus of dispute. Palm Beach Post.

McKinnon, Ken. (July 24, 1980). Seminoles to lobby for funds to attend School. Palm Beach Post.

Meltzer, Milton. (1972) Hunted Like a Wolf, The Story of the Seminole War. Pineapple Press, Inc. .

Osceola, Laura Mae. Interview. Interviewer Mitchell, Virgina. Seminole Tribe of Florida

Osceola, Laura Mae, Interview. (June 24, 1962) Cypress, Billy, Interviewer. Southeastern Indian Oral History Project University of Florida.

Reddy Takes Job with Seminoles, Sunshine News Service, Florida Power and Light Company. Magazine, February 1956

Seminole Tribe of Florida. On The Path to Self-Reliance. 26 min. (1989). Videotape. Subcommittees of the Committees on Interior and Insular Affairs. Termination of Federal Supervision over certain Tribes of Indians. 83rd Cong., 2nd Sess., 1954. S. Doc 2747. H.R. 7321. pt. 8

Snow, Alice Micco and Susan Enns Stansc M, Healing Plants, Medicine of the Florida Seminole Indians, Gainesville: University Press of Florida, 2001, pp. 20-21

Staff, (November 21, 1956). Seminoles yielding to white man as Children integrate into Schools. St. Petersburg Times.

Staff, (November 7, 1949) First In History, Two Seminoles Married Under White Man's Law. The Miami Herald.

Tiger, Betty Mae and West, Patsy. (2001) A Seminole Legend, The Life of Betty Mae Tiger Jumper. University Press of Florida.

Van Camp, April Cone, B.A. (2008). Memories and Milestones: the Brighton Seminole Tribe of Florida and the Digitization of Culture. pp.146. Doctorate dissertation, College of Arts and Humanities, University of Central Florida,

Weaver, Jay and Morgan, Curtis. (May 21, 2010). Target of IRS inquiry. The Miami Herald.

Winters, Milo Mrs., (May 1962). Education and progress of the Florida Seminoles. Daughters of the American Revolution Magazine. (pp 491-492).

West, Patsy. (2010) From Hard Times to Hard Rock, Article on progressive history and adaptability of the Seminole Indians of Florida. Florida Humanities Council

West, Patsy. (1998)The Enduring Seminoles, from Alligator Wrestling to Casino Gaming. University Press of Florida.

West, Patsy. "Reflections" Historical Series, Seminole Tribune Newspaper. Numbers 86, 87, 88, 89 in a series At Home on the Res

1924 Indian Citizenship Act (43 U.S. Stats. At Large, Ch. 233, p. 253 (1924))

"Friends of the Seminoles" organized by Ivy Stranahan and Erma Abbey was chartered as a Florida Corporation in Fort Lauderdale, FL on November 28, 1949. Corporation Book 13, Broward County, pp. 616-622. Office of the Comptroller Broward County, Florida.

Florida, Statutes, 285.061. Some 28,000 acres of this state reservation land in Palm Beach and Broward Counties was transferred to the federal government to be held in trust status for the Seminole Tribe. Legislation was also enacted allowing the tribe to develop the land without interference from the various counties.

U.S. Statutes at Large, Vol. XXIV, p. 338. The attempt of the Dawes Commission to transform the American Indian into yeoman farmers through a series of acreage allotments, all but destroyed the traditional tribal patterns of communal land ownership. It also opened some forty million acres of former Indian lands for settlers.

www.ingramcontent.com/pod-product-compliance
Lightning Source LLC
Chambersburg PA
CBHW071235020426
42333CB00015B/1479